ARISTOCRAT
IN
BURLAP

ARISTOCRAT

IN

BURLAP

A History of

the Potato in Idaho

by

James W. Davis

Published by the Idaho Potato Commission
Fourth Printing Dec. 1992

FOREWORD

A history of the Idaho potato industry must necessarily be different from histories of wars, politics, people and nations even though all of these have had their affect. The history of Idaho® potatoes involves such unlikely events as a man sifting through the soil of his garden for one lost pod from a potato plant, volcanic eruptions that took place in Western America millions of years ago and the development of highly sophisticated pumps that can lift water from great depths in the earth to irrigate potato fields.

In certain ways the mighty Snake River is the mother of Idaho's potato industry. It has, through the centuries, transported and deposited much of the silt that farmers cultivate today in lower lying fields along the river course. It provides much of the water that makes possible the growing of a plant that needs a soil moisture of eighty percent for ideal growth. As it plunges a mile downward in elevation along its course, the Snake generates electrical energy that makes pumping from deep wells possible, and most of the potato growing areas in the state lie contiguous to the Snake River Valley as it twists its way in a 550-mile arc across southern Idaho.

Although natural history has greatly affected the Idaho potato industry, the vision, the decisions and the hard work of thousands of people have, in the end, made possible the establishment, growth, promotion and the future of the industry. The visionaries, the gamblers, the innovators and the leaders stand tall in shaping the development of the industry and their names have a place in its history.

Unfortunately time has taken most of the pioneers, and the information of their struggles, discoveries, triumphs and disappointments must come from family members and what documentation is available. Like all histories, this one searches for the milestones, the unusual, the significant and must by necessity omit persons and events that have played parts of importance.

Individuals who have additions or corrections to make may send their information and documents to the Idaho Potato Commission for possible inclusion in later revisions of this history of the Idaho potato industry.

Acknowledgments

The author of *Aristocrat In Burlap* would like to express sincere appreciation to many people for help and assistance during the original compilation of this book and to others who contributed information for this revised and updated edition. To make a complete list of all the people to whom we are indebted would take too much space here, but they were very necessary to the story.

Much of the book was "written" by people who will never read it. As the words were put down on paper explaining their actions of many-days-past, we couldn't help but admire their devotion to the idea that the potato was a "great agricultural product" for the state of Idaho. For without these people, our story would just be beginning.

There are some people who helped with information and material that must be noted.

Taped interviews proved a very good way to assimilate information. Our special thanks to Ronald Ball, Ken Bergquist, Bob Brown, Gerry Christensen, Harry Fitch, Lester Golden, John Greenlee, R. Keith Higginson, Emil Johnson, Jim Kraus, Edd Moore, Allen Noble, J. R. Simplot, Walter Sparks, and Winslow Whiteley.

We also appreciated the assistance of Leonard Arrington, Mrs. Merle Clayville, Harold Hampton, Mrs. Rolland Jones, Dr. Ed Owens, R. H. Seymour and Mikel Williams. Special thanks are also due Nikki Stilwell who contributed to the original version.

The search for pictures was greatly facilitated by the Idaho Historical Society, Union Pacific Railroad, the University of Idaho, the J. R. Simplot Company and the historical department of the Church of Jesus Christ of Latter-day Saints, Salt Lake City, Utah.

Table of Contents

ARISTOCRAT
IN
BURLAP

xi

Chapter I

SPALDING GROWS THE FIRST IDAHO® POTATOES

The history of the Idaho potato industry logically begins with the growing of the first potatoes within the borders of what is now the Gem State. About this particular event, there is no controversy. It is well documented as to time and place. Where the question does arise is in its importance to the later development of the industry since no potatoes are now grown in the area where these first plantings were made and agriculture was not established on a continuing basis as a result of the first growing of potatoes in Idaho.

Idaho's first potato grower was not a farmer at all, but a Presbyterian missionary, Henry Harmon Spalding. Had he been seeking a life in Idaho as a farmer, the chances are good that he would have found land more suitable to agriculture rather than the locale at Lapwai where he established his mission in 1836 to bring Christianity to the Nez Perce Indians. Although his plan was to choose a location where he could demonstrate to the Nez Perce that they could provide food for themselves through agri-

1

culture rather than hunting and gathering, staying within the domain of the Nez Perce nation limited his choice.

In 1837 the buffalo herds were beginning to be depleted by market hunting and encroachment on their natural domain. Spalding was astute enough to see that the lifestyle of the Indians was changing and that they would soon need other sources of food. By offering to teach them how to raise agricultural crops, he added an additional benefit to the white man's religion that helped gather the Nez Perce around his Lapwai mission.

Historian Clifford Merrill Drury described the Lapwai location as follows: "The Nez Perce had chosen a site for a mission station on the Lapwai Creek, which empties into the Kooskoosky or Clearwater about ten miles above the mouth of the Clearwater. As the party went up along the banks of the Clearwater, Spalding's heart grew heavier and heavier. He wanted a broad flat plain for farming purposes. And there along the Clearwater, the hills rose to an elevation of about 2,700 feet on either side, and crowded down upon the river. How could one farm there?"

In his own journal, Spalding gave the following description. "However, the appearance of the country for the last half day greatly discouraged us. It was very mountainous and broken; the valleys were narrow and without good soil. As we drew near the place we were still more discouraged . . . ."

About ten miles from the mouth of the Clearwater they entered a large valley on the south side of the river, through which the Lapwai Creek ran. The valley was wide

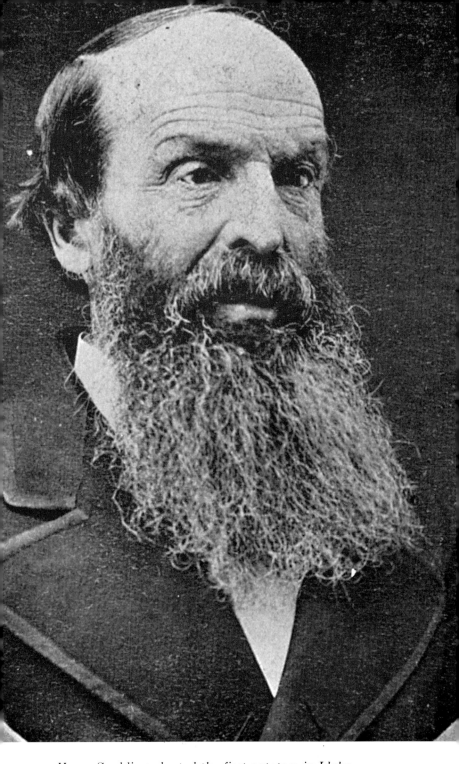

Henry Spalding planted the first potatoes in Idaho.

enough for cultivation, with about half-a-mile between the foothills. There was some small timber along the creek. About two and one-half miles up the creek from its mouth, the missionaries found a site that promised sufficiently good soil.

Drury tells about the beginnings of Idaho agriculture: "Shortly before starting for the north Spalding had tried some of his eastern horses at plowing. To his disappointment, he found that they were not sufficiently recovered from the hard trip over the mountains to do the work. Describing this experience . . . he said: 'The Indians saw my difficulty and said "let not your heart cry. Give us hoes and we will break all the ground you need."' So Spalding distributed about thirty hoes and told them to work a week for him and two weeks for themselves. He also agreed to furnish seed.

By the first of May the Indians had cultivated and planted fifteen acres for themselves. Spalding found it discouraging and difficult work and soon realized that he could not hope to plant one hundred acres, as he had first planned. The Indians had never done any cultivating and knew nothing of the simplest principles of agriculture. Many of the Indians placed implicit trust in Spalding's declaration that the fruits of the soil would make them independent of the hunt, and refrained from going after their annual supply of game .

Spalding sowed two bushels of peas and planted seven bushels of potatoes on the land which was cultivated for him. The balance of the seed he gave to the Indians. He also planted a large assortment of garden vegetables and set out a nursery of apple trees. The true beginning of agriculture and horticulture in Idaho was there at Lapwai."

Neither Spalding nor Whitman, a Methodist missionary at Waiilatpu, raised sufficient food supplies during 1837 to supply fully their needs before another harvest could be gathered. In a letter on May 10, 1839, Whitman told of the problem, "Mr. Spalding and myself were unable to eat potatoes before the last year. The first crop was almost an entire failure, and though I had a tolerable crop the demand was so great for seed I could afford but few for eating."

The summer of 1838 was more favorable and Mother Nature abundantly blessed their efforts. On September 11 Spalding reported that between seventy and eighty Nez Perce families were cultivating the soil. Some raised as much as 100 bushels of potatoes. Spalding estimated his own crop of potatoes at 800 bushels with a value of about eighty English pounds or $388.

A visitor who later observed one of Spalding's potato harvests commented, "Mr. Spalding has a fine lot of potatoes; and I think he will have at least 1,500 bushels, 500 to the acre. I never saw any that turned out so well."

The Indians themselves probably consumated the first commercial sale of Idaho grown potatoes when they found that hungry immigrants traveling in the wagon trains would trade clothing and other goods that the Indians wanted for fresh potatoes.

Log cabins were standard housing in Spalding's day.

Although Spalding succeeded to some extent as a farmer, the missionary work proved to be before its time. Discontent developed among the Indians which resulted in the historic Whitman massacre. The Spaldings were forced to leave Lapwai in 1850 and so ended the first chapter on potato growing in Idaho.

Chapter II
PIONEERS ESTABLISH
FARMS IN
FRANKLIN COUNTY

In the last half of the 19th century, a flood tide of settlers pushed westward. Although the immigrants came to western America for various reasons, it was the farmers who were destined to make a lasting impression on the new land. The gold miners came and went as the fur trappers before them had done and the soldiers and adventurers in their day. It remained for the farmers and cattlemen, however, to put down permanent roots and establish communities which have endured to the present day.

Brigham Young had brought his Mormon pioneers to the Salt Lake Valley where they immediately set about the establishment of their farms. According to Richard Jensen of the L.D.S. Church Historical Department, the manuscript history of Brigham Young on July 24, 1847, states: "About noon, the five acre potato patch was plowed when the brethren commenced planting their seed potatoes."

The first irrigation in the Salt Lake Valley was for the

benefit of the newly planted potatoes. A week later it was evident that the potatoes were growing, according to General History, July 31, 1847.

As the numbers of Mormon colonists in the Salt Lake Valley increased, they pushed outward seeking new lands. In a sense, the first permanent white settlement in Idaho was an accident. The L.D.S. farmers had been directed to establish a new colony north of the Salt Lake Valley area in the Cache Valley. Believing they were still in Utah, the parties selected a site which turned out to be across the state line in Idaho. As their predecessors had in Utah, the new families of settlers began immediately to establish their farms. Here, again, potatoes were one of the first items the farmers planted. William Goforth Nelson was one of the first settlers at Franklin and he recorded the following about the activities of the colony in the summer of 1860: "We all camped in our wagons the first summer, but we had all got homes built by winter; these houses were built in the present meetinghouse lot in a fort. I spent the summer working on ditches, canyon roads, and hauling poles and wood from the canyon. I raised thirty-three bushels of potatoes, which is all that was raised in Franklin that summer except a few onions."

This is the first recorded planting of potatoes in Idaho in an area where the settlers remained and the crop is still grown to some extent today. The planting was accomplished three years before the Idaho Territory was organized.

Of utmost importance to the potato industry was the

discovery of gold in Idaho in 1860. Much of the early potato production was used to feed miners and fields of potatoes were grown to accommodate the men in lead, gold and silver camps located in the Wood River District, Silver City and the Boise Basin.

As early as 1875, the Mormons were shipping potatoes to California. The **Deseret Evening News** of December 2, 1875, reprinted an article from the **San Francisco Chronical** titled "Brigham's Potatoes": "That the farmers of Utah (and Idaho) can hope to compete with the potato raisers of this state, when the rates of freight are taken into consideration, would seem absurd were it not for the fact that the 'co-op' is the parent of an innumerable number of little 'co-ops' scattered all through the Territory, and that the whole is connected and banded with the Church government in such a manner as to give the main institution peculiar facilities for gathering cheaply the products of Utah (and Idaho) soil.

"This is said to be the first speculation — if a Gentile term can be applied to a venture of the inhabitants of Zion — undertaken in this particular community, and it is a bold one. Over 2,000 sacks have already reached this city, and 100 car loads more, sixty of which are on the way, are coming. The potatoes are known as the Neshannock, and it is, of course, claimed that they possess some particular excellence which those of California growth lack."

Again on January 20, 1876, **Deseret Evening News** reported: "During the past season Z.C.M.I. (Zion's Co-operative Merchantile Institution) shipped to San Fran-

The irrigation shovel was symbolic of early western farming.

Early settlers relied on the blacksmith to keep horses shod.

cisco, Cal. — 2,571,466 pounds of potatoes, which cost, delivered at Ogden, $23,045.10. This is a fair commencement, being but the inaugural season of the potato trade with California. This branch of exportation to California was solely conducted by Z.C.M.I., no other house having engaged in it."

Early Idaho newspapers encouraged growing potatoes and the **Idaho Tri-Weekly Statesman** of October 27, 1881, even went so far as to suggest "evaporation" so that fruit and vegetables could "reduce to one-fourth of their original bulk and lower the cost of hauling the product to markets."

"A bushel of potatoes weighs sixty pounds," the newspaper states, "and by this process (evaporation) it can be condensed to thirteen pounds at an expense of about nine cents per bushel. At present it costs two cents per pound to haul a bushel of potatoes from Boise City to Hailey, a distance of 144 miles. This is $1.20 per bushel. But if you evaporate the water and condense your bushel of potatoes into thirteen pounds of bulk, your freight is but twenty-six cents or a clear savings of eighty-five cents upon your bushel of potatoes."

Z.C.M.I. had connections in the Mormon settlements of southern Idaho. One assumes that Idaho settlements must have supplied part of the potatoes for export. The Utah Northern Railroad which connected Franklin with Salt Lake City provided good connections.

An article in the **Deseret News** of February 3, 1888, indicates that Utah (and presumably Idaho as well) had,

12

prior to that time, shipped some potatoes to the eastern market, probably by way of Chicago.

The spread of potato agriculture in eastern Idaho was only a matter of time. Henry E. Jenkins was a freighter, hauling cargo from Lorrine, Utah, to Virginia, Montana, with teams of oxen in 1870. As reported by his daughter, Mrs. John A. Rassmussen of Idaho Falls, in the spring of that year Jenkins hauled a load of potatoes from Farmington, Utah, to Blackfoot, Idaho. The recipient of the shipment was Judge Stephens, who was encouraged by the freighter to plant the potatoes believed to be the first planting in the Blackfoot area. At that time, Idaho Falls was known as Eagle Rock, and a man named John Anderson had built a toll bridge across the Snake River which was utilized by Jenkins in his freighting operation.

Jenkins was apparently on hand in the fall when the potatoes were harvested and reported that they were "as hard as rocks." In spite of this apparent lack of quality in the first crop planted in the Blackfoot area, it did not discourage the early farmers as additional plantings were made in the vicinity. More and more potatoes were planted and the Blackfoot area has grown now into one of the principal potato producing areas in Idaho.

The United States Department of Agriculture estimates were first made for the state of Idaho in 1882 and that year they recorded that 2,000 acres were harvested at the average price of $1.67. The total value of the potato market in Idaho that first year was $250,000.

It was in 1904 when the value of potatoes in Idaho went

over the million mark with $1,328,000. The price average for the season was down from that first year by sixty-two cents, but the 17,000 acres harvested made the difference.

The harvest was 33,000 acres when the potato value was estimated at more than three million dollars in 1915. The unit price was sixty-five cents that year and the following year advanced to $1.32 and the potato industry recorded a seven million dollar value on 33,000 harvested acres of potatoes.

In 1885 after the Oregon Short Line Railroad was completed across southern Idaho, the Boise newspaper was encouraging Idahoans to plant potatoes by calling the attention of farmers to the "possible advantages of raising potatoes for the eastern market."

In 1890 Idaho was admitted to the Union as the forty-third state. And by fall of 1890 Idaho® potatoes were becoming well known in produce circles. Frank Drake of Hailey was awarded $125 as a prize for the third heaviest yield of one acre of potatoes in the United States! Drake was a prominent rancher living just out of Hailey and he also developed a seed potato which was claimed to be the "most prolific known." Drake decided to name it "The Idaho" but the *Wood River Times* of October 17, 1890, decided it would always be called "Drake's Idaho."

And then came news that Thomas Wend of Shoup had received a $100 award offered by a Philadelphia seed dealer for the heaviest potatoes raised from seed purchased from him in 1890. The six potatoes weighed 17 pounds.

"A Complete, Comprehensive Description of the

14

Agricultural, Stock Raising and Mineral Resources of Idaho" compiled from the latest reports of 1891 was a promotional effort of the Union Pacific Railway. The "Diversity of Idaho Agriculture" chapter states that "potatoes yield abundantly, averaging over 200 bushels to the acre, equal to the finest grown in Utah, varying in price from $1 to $3 per 100 pounds, according to the season. When they are well watered, they are of large size, white, mealy and delicious. Many thousand car loads of potatoes were shipped from Idaho points over the Union Pacific Railway in 1887, 1888 and 1890, to eastern markets, where they are in great demand."

According to a Union Pacific Railway booklet, Lemhi County was famous for superior quality potatoes and found a ready market everywhere in the mining camps. "The yield of potatoes in this valley has averaged over 250 bushels to the acre, and the market price varies from $1.50 to $4.50 per hundred pounds . . . the writer has seen some of these tubers weighing four pounds and eight ounces, and was assured by the producer that he had bushels of the same kind in the field, all sound and solid potatoes. During the seventeen years in which Lemhi Valley has been farmed, no failure of this crop has ever been reported."

These first Idaho settlers were pioneers mentally as well as geographically because they had the initiative and willingness to better their conditions regardless of physical hardships and uncertain futures.

In the river valleys, where water was easily diverted,

and with the rich volcanic-ash soil, these hearty people raised a few more potatoes than they needed and found that the extra potatoes resulted in a good cash crop. From this small beginning, Idaho's farmers set out on the conquest of the potato markets of the United States.

Chapter III
LUTHER BURBANK
"FATHERS"
THE IDAHO® POTATO

Nearly all of the potatoes grown within the borders of the state of Idaho are one variety, the Russet Burbank. Although potato breeders have been working for more than forty years in the state in an attempt to improve the Russet Burbank variety, to date, no variety has been introduced that has proven a serious contender to this traditionally famous Idaho baker.

It is fortunate that scientists are in the habit of keeping journals and records of their experiments and work because it is from Luther Burbank's journal that we find the following account of the origin of the Burbank potato.

In 1872 Luther Burbank found a single fruit (seed ball) growing in his New England garden planting of the potato variety Early Rose. Because Early Rose did not commonly set fruits, he watched this fruit throughout the season with an eye to harvesting it when mature. Unfortunately the fruit disappeared from the parent stem. Burbank decided that it would not have been attractive as food to bird or animal and started to look for it. He said, "so day

17

*Luther Burbank, the developer of the famous Idaho®
potato*

after day I returned and took up the search again and at last, this patient search was rewarded. The missing seed ball was found."

Luther Burbank found only twenty-three seeds in the fruit. When the spring of 1872 came, he planted the twenty-three seeds in the garden "as one would plant the seeds of beets or cabbage. The ground had been prepared with great care and each seed was placed about a foot from its neighbor in the row, but no special protection was given the seeds."

All twenty-three seeds grew and produced tubers. Two seedlings appeared better than the Early Rose parent and one of the two was distinctly better in yield and size of tubers. This better seedling proved itself in the summer of 1874. Burbank felt that this new seedling, which would produce two or three times as much as ordinary varieties, should be introduced to the public.

He said that the first dealer to whom he offered the new potato "declined it rather curtly." Burbank finally mustered up enough courage to try again. To bring the potato to the attention of J. H. Gregory of Marblehead, Massachusetts, he sent him a sample by way of introduction. Burbank wanted $500 for the potato, but Gregory would pay only $150. Luther Burbank used the money to move to California. He took with him ten tubers that Gregory allowed him to keep. Gregory named the variety Burbank Seedling (which subsequently became simply Burbank).

The ten tubers which Burbank took with him to California appeared to be the nuclear stock for the introduction of the Burbank variety to the West Coast states. By 1906 over six-million bushels of Burbanks were produced in these states. As late as 1949, 37,517 bushels of certified seed of Burbank were produced in California, Oregon and Washington.

The fact that Burbank subsequently grew more than one-half million seedlings from a deliberate hybridization program without producing another successful variety is also of interest.

The potato which Idaho made famous was not exactly a Burbank. The Burbank variety is a smooth-skinned long white potato and the Russet Burbank variety, which Idaho grows, has a slightly rough reticulated skin commonly termed netted as a Netted Gem, a common synonym for Russet Burbanks.

According to Luther Burbank the Russet Burbank was originated by a man in Denver, Colorado, who evidently selected a chance sport out of Burbank. Burbank stated that,"These Burbank potatoes raised by Lon D. Sweet of Denver, Colorado, have modified their coat in a way that does not add to their attractiveness. It is said, however, that this particular variant is particularly resistant to blight, which gives it exceptional value."

Although "blight" was a rather general term that could be applied to a numerous array of conditions, as used by Burbank in his 1914 writings, the truth is that the Russet Burbank does have considerable resistance to a number of potato tuber diseases. The appearance of the russet mute or sport in the Burbank variety has tended to be somewhat obscure and writers have elected to site the origin as unknown. When Burbank and Russet Burbank are grown together their differences are almost nil. The russeting of the tuber seems to be the major observable difference. The russet mutation appears to involve only the outer layers of the tuber.

Mutation from the russeted mutation back to the original smooth-skin Burbank type has been observed. The smooth-skinned reverse mutant appears to be indistinguishable from the original Burbank variety.

There appears to be no reason to doubt that Russet Burbank variety originated as a periclinal somatic mutation or sport of the Burbank variety as selected by Luther Burbank in the summer of 1873 from twenty-three seedlings derived from a chance fruit on a plant of Early Rose variety.

Luther Burbank, in his writings, has stated that this chance seedling constituted his first commercially valuable plant development and that it furnished a practical means of his moving to California where he was able to carry out his experiments on a far more comprehensive scale than would have been possible in his native New England.

Burbank gained his great renown from his subsequent work in plant hybridization, not from the potato bearing his name. In retrospect, considering the importance of the Russet Burbank potato variety in present day agriculture and industry, the Burbank and subsequent Russet Burbank mutant would appear to be his greatest single accomplishment.

Even though the Burbank strain was developed in New England and mutated in Colorado, it remained for Idaho growers to make the variety famous. Potato scientists have speculated that it was not the Russet Burbank that made Idaho famous, but rather Idaho that made the Russet Burbank famous. The rationale for this statement is based on the fact that Idaho growing conditions tend to produce a superior potato of any variety.

Since potatoes were originally a high altitude plant, they tend to grow better at elevations somewhat above sea level. Summer days along the Snake River Valley in Idaho are sunny and warm. Photosynthesis creates carbohydrates in the green leaves of potato vines in the form of starch. However, the leaves cannot store the starch and a process called translocation takes place. This action requires cool temperatures between sunset and sunrise for the successful transfer of the starch from leaves to tubers. Idaho's climate of warm days and cool nights provides ideal climatic conditions for the growing and production of potatoes.

In addition to climate, potatoes require a high moisture content in the soil. It is thought that the ideal water content is around eighty percent. Most areas where there is sufficient sunshine to grow a good crop of potatoes do not have rainfall providing frequent rain storms to maintain the soild moisture at the ideal level. Since nearly all of south Idaho agriculture depends on irrigation, it is possible for growers to regulate the amount of water and

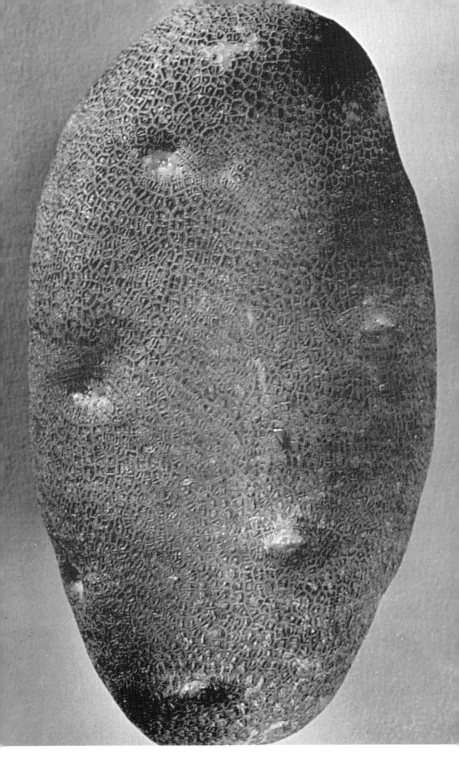

The Russet Burbank is elongated with rough skin.

the soil moisture content at the ideal level.

The third factor that contributes to the quality of potatoes grown in Idaho is the nature of the soil itself. Potatoes seem to grow better in a light soil, like volcanic ash conditions which exist in Idaho's potato growing areas. Not only is the light soil conducive to good potato culture, but a rich supply of trace minerals in the volcanic soil seems to be necessary for successful potato production.

It has never been determined exactly what the soil contains that makes an outstandingly successful potato crop. When new land is brought under cultivation after centuries of "desert" conditions where sagebrush, bitterbrush and a variety of grasses and forbes have been its only production, the first year usually produces an exceptionally fine crop. These desert soils are hardly ever high in nitrogen, and it is necessary to supply the needed nitrogen with chemical fertilizers. Phosphate is also usually added and in some areas, potash seems to produce added yields and quality. These three primary plant foods are replenishable at required rates, but it never seems possible to duplicate the first year crop when the potatoes are planted for the first time in desert soil and all of the trace minerals and native organisms are present.

The net result of Idaho growing conditions is a potato which is high in solids content, has a white,mealy texture when cooked and a pleasing potato flavor.

Although potatoes can be grown in both alkaline and acidic soils, the Idaho farmland is predominantly alkaline. Although potatoes tolerate the alkaline soil balance quite well, it creates another problem—potato scab. It was in fact potato scab that made the Russet Burbank popular in Idaho and in the opinions of some people, the savior of the Idaho potato industry. Since the scab organism grows and prospers only in alkaline soils, in production areas where soils are predominantly acidic, scab is not a problem. It had become a problem of considerable magnitude in Idaho in the early 1900s when farmers were growing Rural New Yorker, Early Rose, Cobbler, Russet Rural, Idaho Rural and Bliss Triumph varieties. The scab organism stays in the soil and when tubers are infected they are worthless for food purposes.

It is not known for sure who brought the first quantities of Sweet's russeted Burbank potatoes to Idaho. It seems instead that several small quantities made their appearance almost simultaneously and various Idaho growers tried the new variety and found that it had considerable resistance to potato scab as well as other diseases.

It took Idaho growers a considerable period of time to learn how to grow the Russet Burbank because it seemed to be extremely sensitive to soil moisture conditions, soil temperatures and the ratio of vines to tubers. Although the consumer and the restaurant chef wanted the smooth, elongated, russeted tuber that pleases the eye and the palate of the final consumer, growers found russets growing knobby, misshapen and ugly at the slightest provocation.

25

They soon found that they could not allow russet potatoes to get dry during the growing season, nor could they grow them with wide plant spacing which allowed too great a vine in relation to the tubers beneath the ground. Russets proved prone to production of knobs, second growth, growth cracks and dumbbell-shaped potatoes compared to round varieties such as Cobblers and Bliss Triumphs. When grading standards were established, tubers with knots to be clipped off became twos and anything that was too rough for the simple clipping operation became a cull. It was therefore necessary for growers to acquire a great deal of knowledge and employ their skill without interruption throughout the growing season to have a quality crop.

The very sensitivity of the Russet Burbank may have been an advantage to Idaho since it was responsible for growers and shippers thinking in terms of potato quality. The late Joe Marshall was one of the crusaders for quality production in Idaho, and was one of the people instrumental in getting a certified seed program started. Reaction by consumers was overwhelmingly favorable.

Never before had a variety of potato appeared that baked with the white and mealy characteristics of the Idaho® russet potato.

For many years Idaho was the only potato growing area of any size that produced Russet Burbank potatoes and that gave Idaho the reputation for being the source of the world's greatest bakers. Growing areas in other states of lower elevation where nighttime temperatures are low enough tended to produce potatoes of lower solid content and with various internal problems that produce darkening and discoloration. States with growing areas above Idaho in elevation had shorter growing seasons and were unable to mature a crop of russets or produce tuber sizes that made them economically feasible. Higher growing areas also tended to produce a slimmer shaped tuber with a pointed end which was less acceptable for a quality potato.

Many of the growing problems have been solved in other states, and considerable acreage of russets are now grown in Washington, Oregon, Colorado, Wisconsin, Michigan and Maine, to mention a few. Idaho potato industry people very sincerely feel that russets grown in other producing areas have never quite achieved the quality that Burbank's famous development has achieved in the state of Idaho.

It is interesting that the accidental finding of a seed pod in Burbank's New England garden had such a remarkable effect on Idaho agriculture. The persistence of Luther Burbank in returning again and again to search for the single seed pod was the factor that held in balance the future of the Idaho potato industry. Certainly the contribution of Luther Burbank, the great plant breeder, to Idaho agriculture is one of astronomical size and very difficult to measure.

Chapter IV
UNIVERSITY OF IDAHO
UNDERTAKES
POTATO RESEARCH

In 1911, soon after Idaho farmers had begun to direct the strong flow of the Snake River to their own farms and fields, they discovered that irrigated land required an entirely new type of farming. They brought their problems to the University of Idaho's Agricultural Experiment Station at Moscow, which had been in existence as a land-grant college since 1892.

It soon became obvious that the establishment of branch stations, strategically located, were needed for research and demonstration in these newly-developed farming areas.

When university officials started looking for a location in the upper Snake River Valley, the Aberdeen area was the scene of considerable reclamation activity. Nearing completion was the canal system of the Aberdeen Valley Land Development Company, the first privately financed reclamation project to be initiated in Idaho under the Carey Act of 1894. In addition the desert area west of the reclamation project was being homesteaded by farmers who were interested in dry farming if suitable crops could be found. Therefore, Aberdeen seemed ideal for the establishment of an experiment station where both irrigated and dry farm crops and techniques could be studied.

During their visits to Aberdeen, the university officials met members of the Aberdeen Commercial Club. Negotiations between the two eventually resulted in the establishment of an experiment station at Aberdeen.

The original eighty acres for the Aberdeen Research Experiment Station were cut diagonally by the Oregon Short Line right-of-way, leaving approximately fifteen acres of land to the west for irrigated fields and the balance of the farm to the east for dry farm crops.

Many Aberdeen residents and local farmers donated labor during the construction and land-clearing phases in the winter of 1911-1912. Actual construction started shortly after the middle of October in 1911. The first buildings were completed during the week of March 23, 1912.

From the start, the experiment station was operated jointly by the University of Idaho and the United States Department of Agriculture. However, management and ownership has transferred slowly to the University of Idaho.

The first year, the experiments with potatoes were considered the most successful and still more than sixty years later, potatoes are the most important crop in terms of the number of research projects being conducted.

Two of the earliest experiments concerning potatoes involved the distance between each plant and between

An early view of Aberdeen experiment station.

Early researchers did their share of hard work.

each row, and the size of the seed piece.

According to the annual report of 1914, the potatoes were planted by hand in furrows made by using a plow. "Accurate planting was insured by using a tape with distances marked off by use of strings tied at proper distances marked on the tape. . . . The potatoes were harvested with a Pugh digger, stored in the new potato cellar and sorted after other fall work had been finished. Sorting was done by hand over a machine especially constructed for the purpose. The ordinary potato sorter was not used on account of bruising the tubers."

The results secured from the distance-in-row experiment were most interesting in that they showed that cut potatoes planted at distances up to and including twenty inches apart in the row gave greater yields of marketable tubers than whole tubers planted at these distances.

The best yield of marketable tubers secured from the cut seed came from seed planted fifteen inches apart in the row, above this and below this the yield of marketable tubers decreased.

The first year that there was an appropriation for specialty work in the field of potato research, James Kraus was hired to work at Aberdeen. During those early years, experiments were concerned with the seed piece sizes, potato cellars, cold storage regulated temperature, bruising and fertilizer and phosphorus levels. Dr. Kraus eventually became the dean of the College of Agriculture at the university.

One of Kraus' principal projects at the Aberdeen Center

in those early days was to research the cause of knobs on russet potatoes. Experimentation showed that it was a top-tuber ratio problem where too many leaves were feeding starch into too few tubers. It was discovered that planting seed closer together to reduce the number of leaves substantially curbed the problem.

The development of a foundation seed program was a major contribution to the industry by the Aberdeen station. Seed is grown under controlled conditions resulting in four plants isolated in a growing situation. If any one of the four plants shows any sign of disease, all four plants are destroyed. Groups of plants that show healthy signs are harvested and used for foundation seed. Certified seed has been the answer for controlling many potato diseases including ringrot bacteria and mosaic disease. Foundation seed is certified by the Idaho Crop Improvement Association.

A leading researcher in potato storage practice has been Walter Sparks, a horticulture scientist at the Aberdeen station for more than forty years. His experiments and research papers have made him a well-known authority on the subject. Principles he developed are used in almost all potato storage units today.

The Commission entered into an association with the University of Idaho's Aberdeen Agricultural Experimental Station in 1948, one year after Sparks began his work. The support given the research and education programs of the Aberdeen center by the IPC has been a major factor in the quality and quantity of work that they have been able to accomplish.

Results of the early seed-piece size work indicated that the "tubers cut-in-half yielded the best in every instance and the three-ounce seed cut-in-half were six bushels better in yield than the next highest plot which was the six-ounce seed cut-in-half. The difference in cost of seed, however, would make a much greater difference in income per acre than the above yields would indicate."

In the line of farm equipment improvement, the research center built a potato cellar at a cost of $110 for materials in 1914. All the work in the construction was done by the station staff. The object was to get a maximum amount of safe storage room at a minimum cost and demonstrate to farmers that a cheap but effective storage cellar was possible on every farm where potatoes, beets or other perishable crops were grown for sale or feed.

The following year tests were made on the method of cutting seed and indicated a similarity to those of 1913. The highest yield of marketable tubers was obtained from the plats planted with the stem-end and blossom-end seed pieces. The test was conducted on twentieth-acre plats with six rows in each plat.

In 1916 the first real field day was "staged" at the Aberdeen station. Approximately three-hundred-fifty farmers from southeastern Idaho spent the day inspecting the station plats and securing information regarding experiments being conducted. The superintendent accompanied the visitors about the farm, showing them the various items of interest and explaining results already collected.

One of the major "victories" of the Aberdeen research station has been over ringrot. This disease, which often would destroy an entire potato field or all the potatoes in a single storage unit, now can be controlled by the use of clean seed and good sanitation practices in handling potatoes. One of the major carriers of bacteria of the ringrot organism was discovered to be the cutting knife, which can become infected by one potato and pass the bacteria to the next twenty tubers.

In sorting out some of the major accomplishments of the research center in the area of potatoes, Sparks listed the development of proper management methods for sanitation, correct irrigation practices and the encouragement of farmers to use them, as among the most important. For many years the potato crop was the one taken care of after the wheat was threshed and other crop chores were completed on the farm.

The research center soon learned that to prevent "pointed-nosed" and "bottle-necked" potatoes, the tubers should be watered at the correct times. But there were also many other advantages in taking care of the potato plant at the proper time.

"The work at the research center is never done," according to Sparks. One answer for an inquiring farmer may develop into three or four more questions each needing an answer.

Estimated value of four to ten million dollars per year is measured for work done in saving potatoes in storage

The Joe Marshall Potato Research Center.

Inset; U of I Ag. College Dean, A. Larry Branen, welcomes visitors to the dedication of the U of I storage research building at Kimberly, Idaho. Cutting ribbon, l to r: Gary Lee, asst. dean; Gale Kleinkopf, station supt.; Dean Branen; Jack Parks, IPC chairman; Jeff Raybould, PGI president; Tom Bell, U of I provost, and Larry O'Keefe, plant, soil and entomological sciences head.

cellars alone.

It is the nature of scientific research that, when properly done, all projects produce data and information, but not all research finds solutions to problems. The potato industry in Idaho has contributed generously to the cost of projects seeking solutions to growing problems and to basic research into the fundamental nature of potatoes. The USDA has supplied financial assistance in certain areas and the University of Idaho College of Agriculture has also made substantial contributions.

In reviewing research results over the years it is clear that the financial benefits to the industry that resulted from the R and E programs have far exceeded the total investment by all three contributors.

Professor Walter Sparks evaluates the contributions of U of I research programs to the potato industry in the area of potato storage where he did the major part of his research.

Sparks says that the ability to store potatoes from one crop to the next is probably the greatest research-created benefit in economic terms. It allows Idaho shippers to market fresh potatoes 12 months of the year which is vital in maintaining customer relationships and market share. It also makes it possible for processing plants to operate the full season, which gives the processor a better return on the money he has invested in plant facilities. Workers benefit from the availability of year-round jobs and the communities from the increased economic activity.

Other University research that has made significant contributions to the Idaho® potato industry includes an ongoing program in irrigation practices. Improvements in yield and quality have resulted and savings have been made in preventing the leaching of fertilizers and in more efficient water use.

The virus-free program which has made it possible for seed potato growers to provide seed free of Virus X and Virus Y to commercial growers is another U of I achievement noted by Sparks. The presence of seed-born virus reduces yield and quality.

Partial or complete control of weeds, wireworms, nematodes, verticillium wilt, potato scab, ring rot, Colorado potato beetle, leaf roll and blight have been achieved through the work of the staff of U of I scientists. Without the ability to deal with these cultural problems, Idaho growers would probably be unable to produce an acceptable product at a price consumers could afford.

Research and development in the mechanical handling of potatoes to prevent bruise damage have produced design innovations that have been adapted by the manufacturers of farm equipment. As an example, pilers and harvesters are now designed to minimize drops and rough handling of tubers.

Potato breeding at Aberdeen in a joint USDA-U of I program has resulted in the release of new varieties for potato chips, early processing use and early fresh market sales. To date, however, the one super potato that could equal or exceed the Russet Burbank in quality and be easier and more profitable to grow, has eluded the breeders. Genetic engineering might yet provide the means to achieve that goal by the selective improvement of Luther Burbank's masterpiece.

Extension potato specialists, funded jointly by the U of I and the Idaho Potato Commission, have done much to assist growers with cultural problems and make research information available. The annual potato school sponsored by the University and held each year in Pocatello, which is routinely attended by growers from all over the U. S. and Canada, has also been effective in imparting knowledge gained from research activities.

The grower segment of the industry has always looked hopefully to potato research, including the development of new potato varieties, for solutions to their growing, storage and marketing problems. In 1976 a movement was started to purchase a 120 acre farm, with a sprinkler system already in place, adjacent to the University of Idaho Research and Extension Center at Aberdeen to provide more land for the breeding and variety development program.

The IPC contributed money from research and education funds which was supplemented by a legislative appropriation and the farm was purchased for $360,000. The potato breeding program at Aberdeen was greatly expanded when the new acreage became available.

The most recent addition to Idaho research capability is a state of the art storage facility built in 1991 and located at Kimberly, Idaho. Individual storage bins are completely isolated from each other and provided with environmental controls to simulate any desired storage condition. The building was made possible by industry donated funding and R and E funds from the IPC.

The process of selecting research projects involves the entire Idaho potato industry which makes needs known through the Research and Education Committee. Research proposals submitted by the University of Idaho and other research organizations are evaluated by the R and E Committee which is composed of two IPC members, the Commission executive director and nine people representing major interest areas in the industry.

Members-at-large also sit on the committee at the pleasure of the chairman by reason of specialized areas of knowledge so that they can be called upon for the evaluation of research proposals.

After study and negotiation with research organizations, the R and E Committee makes recommendations to the Idaho Potato Commission which collects research funds as part of the advertising assessment and is responsible to the industry for the use of the money. The IPC can also contract for projects that do not come through the committee.

Research dollars, through the work of the dozens of scientists that have been involved throughout the years, have accomplished a great deal and yield a huge return to the Idaho potato industry for money spent.

Chapter V
JOE MARSHALL
BECOMES LEGENDARY
"IDAHO POTATO KING"

More than anyone else, perhaps Joe Marshall's career paralleled the development of the Idaho potato industry. His tireless energy and his total involvement contributed greatly to his prominence and caused him to be known as the "Idaho Potato King" in trade circles.

Forced to quit school at an early age in his home state of Ohio, Joe Marshall continued his education studying subjects that interested him where and when he could. He had a feeling for civil engineering and became a self-educated civil engineer specializing in the construction of irrigation canals and dams.

He first came to Idaho in 1902. Prior to the opening of the Twin Falls irrigation tract, Joe Marshall had been working for the Milner Brothers who constructed Milner Dam which made the Twin Falls tract possible. His trip to Idaho was to inspect the new irrigation project and he was greatly impressed with the land, the location and the potential of the Magic Valley as a new agricultural area. As a consequence, he filed on a 160-acre tract east of Twin

Falls, a farm operation which is still owned by the Marshall family.

The years between 1902 and 1916 were spent on a variety of engineering and irrigation projects including a period of time when he purchased and developed land in Mexico. He returned to Idaho to construct an earthen dam at Mackay for an irrigation project in that area. The next year he went back to his Twin Falls farming operation and produced a crop of forty acres of potatoes. This was the real start of Joe Marshall's Idaho potato career and was an event that proved to be very influential in the history of the Idaho potato industry.

One of Marshall's greatest personality traits was his ability to attack and solve problems. When trouble developed he looked for the cause and worked out a solution. An example of this was a trip he made to Chicago in 1917 to induce the railroads to make rail cars available for shipments of potatoes from Idaho. While cars were lined up on the siding in Chicago unused, there was a shortage of rolling stock in the western United States to ship Idaho® potatoes to eastern markets. He was successful in talking top freight directors of the Union Pacific Railroad into diverting sufficient rolling stock to Idaho, where it was needed, and solved a car shortage which was creating a disaster in the Idaho potato industry.

Joe Marshall formed a strong identification with the Idaho® potato and with this came a desire to deliver it to the consumer in the very best condition. For this reason he handled the marketing of his own potatoes, doing the

41

Horses were still used in the 1940s to plant potatoes.

Joe Marshall frequently dug in fields to check crop's progress.

sorting and packing in the cellars on his farm. The potatoes were cleaned by brushing, since Marshall believed that washing was a bad practice and tended to deteriorate the quality of the potatoes before they could be delivered to the consumer. He also developed a consciousness of bruising and injury to the tubers very early in his experience. He always insisted that employees handle the potatoes carefully.

Joe Marshall left Idaho in 1919 to construct an irrigation project in Utah and returned in 1921. During these years, the Idaho potato industry had developed some serious problems. It was a common practice to save the small potatoes out of each year's crop for the next year's seed and most of the growers were having disease and quality problems. Coupled with that, prices paid farmers for potatoes had reached a very low point in 1921 and many of the farmers in the Twin Falls area were in serious financial trouble.

A great many of them had mortgaged their farms to banks in the area and the bankers were extremely concerned about the economic condition of the farmers in general. After discussing the situation with several banking organizations, Joe Marshall accepted the responsibility for overseeing the operation of farms on which these banks had mortgages. The banks were anxious to have the farmers prosper, pay back their loans and save their farms. It was Joe Marshall's responsibility to see that the farms were properly operated and that the sincere, conscientious farmers were able to overcome their financial

43

problems.

During this period of time, Joe Marshall not only operated his own farm, but many others as well. He bought a Model-T Ford and constructed a pick-up type box on the back. Traveling constantly from morning to night, he went from one farm to another advising growers on irrigation practices, cultivation, harvesting procedures, storage and all aspects of their farming operation. He urged most of the farmers to grow potatoes, because the potential cash income from the crop offered a solution to the depressed economic conditions in Idaho farming in general.

At this time, Joe Marshall sought a solution to the quality problem which was plaguing the Idaho potato growers. He did some extensive traveling including a trip to Maine to find out, if possible, why the quality of Idaho potatoes had deteriorated. From his experience and the information he was able to gather, he concluded that good quality seed would be a major factor in rescuing the industry. He then started a quest for clean, disease-free seed and was able to find a carload in Montana and an additional quantity in Oregon. He bought these lots and brought them back to Idaho to be used in the production of more seed potatoes.

From one car of seed purchased in Oregon and three that came from Thompson Falls, Montana, he established a seed industry in the Ashton area by encouraging growers there to produce seed potatoes to be sold to the commercial growers to the south. In 1924, he shipped 150 carloads

Marshall and Texas Attorney General at produce convention.

of certified seed potatoes from the Ashton and Driggs area in eastern Idaho where the high altitude and isolation kept disease problems from developing.

Since Joe Marshall was supervising farming operations for the banks, he was able to convince the farmers that the use of specially grown certified seed would be a benefit to them. The practice immediately improved the quality of Idaho® potatoes and put the Idaho producing area ahead of others in the nation as far as the quality of their products was concerned.

During these years Joe Marshall developed some marketing connections in Chicago and established a good reputation for the quality of his Blue Diamond brand potatoes. He personally oversaw the packing and shipping of the potatoes grown on his own farm and the farms that he was supervising for the bank, and his potatoes commanded a premium price wherever they were known and sold.

One year when the prices were particularly low and the average Idaho® potato was bringing forty cents for a hundred-pound bag, Joe Marshall's potatoes brought $1.40 because the customers who knew the brand were willing to pay for the assured quality.

Under Marshall's management, most of the farmers who had been in financial trouble were able to pay off their mortgages and own their farms free and clear.

As Joe Marshall and others became successful in the potato business, the volume of potatoes grown in Idaho increased. With this increase in production came problems in marketing. It was customary, in those days, for many grower-shippers who loaded potatoes in cars in Idaho to start them to market usually with Chicago as a destination or diversion point. Chicago potato dealers bought and resold the Idaho® potatoes, finding homes for them in most of the large cities in the United States. With so much control centralized in Chicago, and more than adequate supplies, the Idaho grower began to have price problems again.

By this time many interested and dedicated people were involved in the growing and shipping of potatoes. While seeking a solution for their problems they established the Idaho Fruit and Vegetable Advertising Commission which later became the Idaho Potato Commission. Joe Marshall was involved in the original concept of the Commission and was a member of that promotion body for more than twenty years.

He especially believed in showing Idaho® potatoes at produce trade conventions and for many years he attended the annual United Fresh Fruit and Vegetable Convention and supplied potatoes for the display that was sponsored by the Idaho Potato Commission.

He spent considerable time prior to the conventions personally selecting potatoes from his own cellars to be displayed for produce jobbers and brokers to see. His philosophy of showing the best merchandise available was summarized by an expression that he frequently used: "you don't take your skim-milk calf to the fair."

Joe Marshall's personal participation in these conven-

Joe Marshall wore his Idaho potato crown at produce conventions.

Joe Marshall inspects quality of potatoes behind digger.

tions as well as the frequent trips he made to marketing areas made him a well-known figure among produce trade people. By this time the Idaho Potato Commission had a well-organized field merchandising program in operation and with the assistance of C. G. Rice and Dean Probert, Joe Marshall became a spokesman for the Idaho potato industry through the columns of newspapers in cities where conventions were held.

Newspaper writers reporting the convention would frequently interview Joe Marshall. Potatoes used in displays were often contributed to orphanages and children's homes following the convention which created local publicity and earned Joe Marshall a reputation as a philanthropist.

It was obvious to people who worked with Joe Marshall that he really loved agriculture and, particularly, the growing of potatoes. In the early days potato fields were small and were irrigated primarily with gravity irrigation. During the growing season Joe Marshall traveled constantly from one field to another personally supervising the growing of the crop. He frequently dug into hills of potatoes to check the condition of the tubers and the progress of development during the growing season. He was always ready to pass on his expertise to other growers and his reputation as a potato expert became widespread throughout the Idaho industry.

Before the days of rubber-coated digger chains and padded handling equipment, Joe Marshall had his equipment wrapped with twine to provide padding and prevent

49

bruising of the tubers. It became a well-known fact among Joe Marshall's employees that anyone who was observed handling potatoes carelessly or bruising them would be instantly unemployed. One cardinal rule in his packing operations was that if a sack of potatoes was dropped, the sack had to be opened and the potatoes sorted to replace damaged or bruised tubers. Marshall felt that the sack of potatoes was on its way to one of his customers and he wanted to be sure that the customer would not be disappointed with the quality in the bag.

Although a trend-setter in the industry, he did not accept everything new. Even when the industry converted for the most part to washing potatoes before packing, Joe Marshall refused to take the step. So strong was his conviction that washing potatoes was a bad practice, he continued to pack his tubers dry as long as he grew and shipped potatoes.

His son, Charles Marshall, went into the potato shipping business on his own, handling potatoes that he grew and the potatoes of many other growers in the area around Jerome, Idaho. He has stated that he was unable to meet the rigid quality standards set by his father and that he never shipped potatoes under any of his father's brands.

With his self-imposed quality standards, Joe Marshall never compromised for the expediency of getting rid of a particular lot of potatoes.

One of the great boosters for the Idaho® baking potato was a Chicago restaurant owner named Dario Toffenetti. Toffenetti stated that he got started buying and serving

Idaho® potatoes because of a particular lot that was in storage in Chicago that nobody wanted to buy.

This lot of potatoes proved to be one that had been shipped by Joe Marshall to Chicago and they were all of exceptionally large size. It was an experimental shipment in which all of the smaller tubers had been removed and probably the lot consisted of potatoes weighing twelve ounces and up.

Toffenetti stated that he went to the warehouse where the potatoes were being stored and they were huge and beautiful.

The idea of serving these large potatoes caught his imagination and he bought the entire shipment. Toffenetti, at that time, was the owner and operator of several restaurants in Chicago and he featured these big Idaho bakers in his restaurants. The reaction of his customers was very gratifying to the Italian restaurant operator and he reported in his charming Italian accent, "and the customers say to me, 'Dario, you serve too much food. I can't eat it all.'" Toffenetti was shrewd enough to realize that a large baked potato on a plate was an inexpensive way to give the customer the impression of extremely generous portions. In the economically depressed days of the '30s everyone was looking for an exceptional value, and the reputation of Toffenetti's generosity was a great promotional device for him.

Toffenetti displayed large Idaho bakers in the windows of his restaurant and made several trips to Idaho where he became acquainted with leaders in the Idaho industry and

51

formed many warm friendships. Toffenetti and Joe Marshall were fast friends and were known to always get together when Marshall was in Chicago or Toffenetti visited Idaho.

Joe Marshall came as close to becoming a legend in the Idaho potato industry as any man. His concepts of the production and marketing of high quality were undoubtly responsible for much of the early advantage that Idaho enjoyed and the reputation that the state built up as a supplier of quality potatoes and the improvement of cultural practices among Idaho growers.

His concepts of seed potato quality were implemented by the University of Idaho in a foundation seed program. Seed growers in the high altitude seed producing areas of the state owe much to Marshall's vision and understanding of the value of certified seed.

His persistence in hanging on to practices that he believed in, contributed much to the color and the legend of Joe Marshall. In his later years, he wore a mustache and was very frequently seen clad in bib overalls. He appeared to wear them proudly as the uniform of a man who has spent his life in agriculture and loved the Idaho potato.

The appreciation expressed for Joe Marshall's contributions in his own time was very gratifying to him in later years and especially the title of "Idaho Potato King," which he always enjoyed and cherished. He died in January, 1964, at the age of 89.

A tribute was paid Joe Marshall when the potato industry research center was established at the University of Idaho Experiment Station at Aberdeen. The modern laboratory office and greenhouse complex became known as the Joe Marshall Research Center. His name appears on the bronze plaque and a color picture of Joe Marshall inspecting a field of blossoming potatoes decorates the wall inside the entrance.

The contribution of men such as Marshall, who worked tirelessly and uncompromisingly for the betterment of the industry, would be extremely difficult to measure. But it is certain that Joe Marshall's contributions have earned for him a prominent place in the history of the Idaho potato industry.

Chapter VI
J. R. SIMPLOT
BUILDS A
POTATO "EMPIRE"

Of the many people whose lives and activities have influenced the direction and progress of the Idaho potato industry, one stands out from all the rest, John (Jack) R. Simplot. Simplot has been in turn the largest fresh shipper of potatoes in the state, the largest grower of Idaho potatoes and the largest processor. And, along with the distinction of being first in Idaho in each of these categories, Simplot probably has the distinction of being "number one" in the world.

Although Jack Simplot has achieved much in the size and the scope of his potato operation, his greatest contribution to the industry has been his immense capacity for innovation, pioneering, speculation and the absolutely fearless assault of unknown frontiers in production and marketing.

J. R. Simplot was not born in Idaho. He traveled to the Gem State in an immigrant car with his father, mother, brothers and sisters. The Simplots went first to Washington, where they soon became dissatisfied, and back tracked to Idaho. Their first year was spent in the farming village of Burley where the older Simplot built several houses. The family occupied one of these houses for a while as their new Idaho home.

This was the time of great new agricultural developments in Idaho and irrigation projects were opening vast new tracts of land. Jack Simplot's father decided to become a part of the homesteading activity and took a tract near Declo, Idaho. The family moved to the farm, built a log house and began the labor of clearing brush and leveling the land to get ready for the availability of irrigation water. Among his earliest recollections, Jack Simplot tells of dragging a railroad rail across the land between teams of horses to tear out the sagebrush and level the land for irrigation. The process was known as railing.

Irrigation water was ready on schedule the next spring and the Simplots planted their first crop including an acreage of potatoes. The Russet Burbank was unknown in Idaho at that time and Simplot recalls that they probably grew Rurals or Cobblers. Farm labor was done primarily with the power of horses and human muscles and Jack Simplot's boyhood was spent in hard work helping his father on the farm.

In fact his first job outside the family operation was hauling potatoes out of the fields for a neighbor and into the town of Declo two miles away. It took three teams of horses to pull a wagonload of bagged potatoes from the field and, once on the highway, two teams continued the trip to town. Under these conditions it was possible to make two trips per day. Wagonloads contained up to 2,400 pounds of potatoes.

The marketing of potatoes for the grower was very unsophisticated at that time. It was necessary for the farmer to load the bags of potatoes on a railroad boxcar, pad and insulate the load with straw, and if the shipment was made in freezing weather, the shipper would accompany the load of potatoes and keep charcoal stoves burning in the car to prevent freezing. The railroad provided a seat in the caboose for the owner of the potatoes and Jack Simplot recalls his father making a trip to Kansas City with such a shipment. His father returned stating that the enterprise had been a disaster. After selling the potatoes in Kansas City, he had only enough money for the cost of the freight and a ticket home.

Despite the difficulties involved, Idaho farmers continued to grow potatoes and were gradually finding some acceptance for them in eastern markets. Young Jack Simplot found the challenge and the enterprise of farming and business more exciting than school and at an early age was growing potatoes on his own on a tract of land that he rented from Lindsey Maggert, at that time the most prominent potato grower in the Declo area.

One of the turning points in the Simplot career came when Jack accompanied Lindsey Maggert and two other friends, the Atchley brothers, on a late season elk hunting trip. The party journeyed by a horse-drawn bobsled up the Warm River to the boundary of Yellowstone Park. The snow fell heavily most of the four or five days that they

Packed in farm cellars, potatoes were shipped from Twin Falls.

World War II dehydrated potatoes were shipped from this plant.

were in the area and Simplot's energy and adventurous spirit were demonstrated when he bagged the quota of elk for the entire party.

As they were journeying back home, Jack recalled that someone was manufacturing an electrically-powered potato sorter in Shelley, Idaho. He discussed the matter with Lindsey Maggert and the two agreed to seek out the factory and have a look at the innovation. They found the shop where the machines were being manufactured. Before leaving, Jack Simplot and Lindsey Maggert had purchased one of the potato sorters in partnership. After the machine had been manufactured it was loaded on a boxcar and shipped to Declo by railroad.

When it arrived, Jack Simplot assembled the machine and found it to be much more efficient than the hand-shaking method that had been used previously. In operation, the sorter was moved into the farmer's cellar and the electrical cord was plugged into a light socket. Potatoes were dumped on a table by a conveyor and as the belt carried them along, the people working on either side of the table sorted out the number ones, the number twos and the culls. The produce was then bagged and hauled to town, loaded in a railroad car and shipped.

The story continued that Jack Simplot sorted his own potatoes first, then those of Maggert, the partner in the operation. He then continued to sort potatoes for other growers, moving the machine and his crew from farm to farm. The sorting activity began to conflict with a business enterprise owned by one of Maggert's friends so, one spring day after a winter of sorting activity, Maggert found Jack and suggested that he close down the operation and get back to his farming. Jack had made commitments to several other growers to sort their potatoes and an argument ensued. The longer the discussion, the more obvious it became that the two were not going to agree, so finally one of them produced a silver dollar and they decided to let chance decide who would own the potato sorter. The coin was flipped and Jack Simplot ended up as the sole owner of the machine which was the beginning of the J. R. Simplot Produce Company.

Once launched in the business of shipping Idaho® potatoes, Simplot saw the advantage of size. He began building and buying shipping warehouses and increasing his annual shipments of Idaho fresh potatoes during the 1930s.

It was during this same period that the Idaho industry was acquiring sophistication, upgrading its equipment and gaining a reputation for quality with the new Russet Burbank variety. As the growing industry wrestled with marketing problems, the desire to gain a larger measure of control over the distribution of their product led Idaho potato industry leaders to form the Advertising Commission in 1937. This, along with the development of consumer packs, sizing, washing, a marketing order and stricter controls over quality, moved the industry into a position of leadership in the potato world. Fresh shipping operations in the '30s in Idaho tended to be small units. With the advent of motor transportation, farm-to-market distances

59

Defects were trimmed from potatoes before dicing and drying.

Jack Simplot poses in potato storage at Caldwell plant.

were less important and shipping operations in central locations became larger. Consolidation began to take place.

Simplot aggressively sought new customers and bought out competitors as the tides of change convinced some shippers to leave the business. Jack Simplot concentrated his energy and ability to innovate in the fresh produce business and by 1940 was the largest single shipper of Idaho® potatoes. He had thirty-two packing warehouses from American Falls to Jamison, Oregon, and in 1940 shipped 10,000 cars of Idaho® potatoes to receivers all over the United States. While his shipping empire was making great strides, Jack Simplot was also active in potato growing. Like other more progressive growers of his time, he tried certified seed and was enthusiastic with the results. Prior to this time he had experienced crop failures when it was impossible to determine what had happened. Most growers were saving small potatoes from the previous year's crop to use as seed for the next season. Bacterial and viral diseases tended to grow worse under this practice and bad hereditary traits were kept in the growing operation rather than being replaced by better strains of seed.

Simplot started a system with growers from whom he bought potatoes. He would buy certified seed and induce each one of his growers to purchase ten or more bags from him on credit. They were instructed to plant these ten bags of potatoes late in the season which caused the tubers to be small in size and relatively immature at

61

harvest time. This lot of potatoes then, which had been grown from the certified seed and multiplied by one year's growing, served as the seed for the next year's crop. The practice, which Simplot developed, proved to be so superior to using "year out" seed that it became almost a universal practice in the potato growing areas of Idaho.

In that period of Idaho agriculture, the use of chemical fertilizers was virtually unknown. Growers provided the nitrogen that was needed for a good potato crop by growing alfalfa hay on the land for two or three years and plowing under the last alfalfa crop. The nitrogen fixing ability of the alfalfa enriched the soil and made possible a potato crop which would yield high enough to be profitable. Some growers, however, tried growing potatoes after potatoes or on a short rotation cycle and found yields and quality falling off to a point where it was not profitable.

Jack Simplot recalls his introduction to chemical fertilizer by remembering one year when he purchased a carload of fertilizer from the Pacific Guano Fertilizer Company of California. The purchase was made from a salesman who was traveling in Idaho and Simplot decided to try one carload as an experiment.

He was using an Iron Age potato planter and anticipating delivery of the fertilizer, he ordered a fertilizer attachment from the manufacturer in North Dakota. The device arrived, the fertilizer was delivered on the siding and he started to plant the crop of potatoes. The material itself was packaged in burlap bags tied at the top with wire. It was unlabeled and of a yellowish color.

When the planting operation began, Simplot found that he could not adjust the fertilizer attachment to apply the plant food at a low enough rate. It became obvious that the carload of fertilizer was not going to cover the entire forty-acre field. After struggling with the device, he finally told the operator to go ahead and use up the fertilizer as far as it went, and plant the rest of the field without the benefit of the new product.

Simplot said that at harvest time he learned one of the most startling lessons of his lifetime. In the portion of the field where the fertilizer had been applied, the crop of potatoes was beautiful. They were large, of good quality, good type and the yield was heavy. Where the fertilizer supply had run out "was where we ran out of potatoes," according to Simplot. The increase in yield and quality was so startling that Simplot became an enthusiastic advocate of the use of fertilizer in growing potatoes. He found it extremely difficult to get anyone to agree with him on recommending fertilizer, but he went about the task with missionary zeal. The fertilizer industry was in its infancy and supplies of nitrogen and phosphate fertilizers were extremely difficult to get. The problem finally led to Simplot's decision to produce his own fertilizer which has become a large and lucrative division of his enterprises.

Having become the largest shipper of fresh produce in Idaho, Jack Simplot was not satisfied. He was looking for additional worlds to conquer. The advent of World War II created new demands and markets. Simplot's attention

63

was called to the fact that his produce company in western Idaho was making sales of Idaho-grown sweet Spanish onions to a customer in California who seemed prepared to pay a good price for the commodity.

Simplot had decided to find out how a California processor could buy onions in Idaho at a high price and still make a profit, so he followed one of the onion shipments to Vacaville, California, where it was consigned to the Basic Vegetable Corporation. Basic Vegetable had a contract from the United States Quartermaster Corps to dehydrate onions for military use. Jack reasoned that if the onions could be shipped to California and dehydrated there, the dehydration could also take place in Idaho at a savings in transportation costs and would probably constitute a new profit source for his business.

He contacted the Quartermaster Corps and they were indeed interested in additional sources of dehydrated onions. Simplot acquired a tract of land west of Caldwell which had the convenient advantage of being in the onion growing area of southwest Idaho and eastern Oregon. The land itself was a flat tract of bottom land south of the Boise River with a high saline content which made it unsuitable for agriculture. It was also located on a railroad branch line that connected Caldwell, Greenleaf and Wilder, Idaho. This site became the home of Simplot's first processing plant, a dehydration facility for onions.

The dehydration of onions started in 1940 and by 1942 during the war the United States Quartermaster Corps was looking for other sources of foods, particularly

Staff meeting in 1943 included, left to right, Ray Dunlap, Harold Pratt, Henry Ankeny, Jack Simplot, Leon Jones, Owen Sproat, Harold Aird and Pares Curtis.

potatoes. Rodgers Brothers Company had dehydrated some diced potatoes in Idaho Falls in 1940, but large-scale drying of the famous Idaho product had not taken place.

Simplot tested the onion dehydration equipment at the Caldwell site for the first runs of dehydrated potatoes and a satisfactory product was produced. From that point on, expansion took place as fast as equipment and materials became available. With more men being called into service every day, a demand for dehydrated food stuffs became greater and greater. Selling food to the government was a profitable business and with the processing operation added to the large Simplot Produce Company, Jack Simplot was emerging as one of the rich, energetic young businessmen of the 1940s.

Simplot had hired a young chemist named Ray Dunlap to operate the quality control department of his potato and onion dehydrator at Caldwell. With war-time production running smoothly, Simplot began to talk with his staff members about the future of potato processing in postwar years. Although dehydrated diced potatoes were satisfactory food stuffs for military use, they were not popular with service men and their postwar future showed little promise.

Dunlap began to experiment with other types of potato processing. He acquired a quick freezing unit and made attempts to freeze potatoes in various forms as a means of preserving them from the processing plants to the consumer. Simplot states that one day Ray Dunlap walked into his office with a sample of French fried potatoes. He asked Simplot to sample them which he did and found them to be of good quality. Dunlap then revealed the fact that the French fries had been frozen, thawed out and reconstituted. Simplot states that this was the beginning of the frozen French fried potato industry and that Ray Dunlap was the inventor of the new product.

Following the war, Simplot enterprises became more diversified and J. R. Simplot moved his offices to Boise, Idaho, 27 miles from the Caldwell plant. It was during this period of time that staff members in Caldwell began developing products for the postwar consumer and experimenting with production line techniques for producing them.

Although postwar dehydrated potato products have assumed an important place in both consumer and institutional distribution, it is frozen potato products that have captured the imagination of the American public and truly revolutionized the use of potatoes. Jack Simplot stated that his initial reaction to the idea of freezing potatoes was that they would turn to water. Freezing of other vegetables, however, was underway by the time Ray Dunlap made his first tests with potatoes. The secret proved to be precooking or blanching which stabilized the potatoes and made it possible to freeze them to be thawed out later without breaking down the cellular structure.

The first Simplot experiments involved simply boiling French cut potato strips and freezing them. These strips could be satisfactorily frozen, thawed and cooked in a French fryer, but they did not have the necessary convenience factor. When Dunlap hit upon the idea of blanching, deep-fat frying and freezing the strips, he had solved the basic problem with the frozen French fries.

In the late 1940s and early '50s, most housewives did not have a deep-fat fryer as part of their kitchen equipment. The advantage of Dunlap's potato was that it could be removed from the carton, spread on a piece of aluminum foil or cookie sheet and heated in the oven. Although the oven-reconstituted French fries were not as good as those heated in a deep fryer, they were of satisfactory quality to be acceptable to the housewife and her family.

When sales efforts were turned to the restaurant and institutional market, the problem of reconstitution was much simpler since most commercial eating establishments already had a French fryer. The advent of frozen French fries greatly increased the capacity of this equipment since it took only approximately three minutes to heat up frozen Frozen fries from the icy state as compared to fifteen minutes required to cook raw potato strips and get them ready for serving. A piece of deep frying equipment could then put out five times the volume during busy times of the day and the quality was significantly better than preparation from raw strips.

Simplot's problem was one of adapting Dunlap's laboratory procedures to production line technique. The same peeling and water blanching equipment that was used for dehydrated diced potatoes could be utilized in the early preparation for frozen French fries. The problem to be solved was the actual deep-fat frying process.

68

Simplot gives credit for the technical breakthrough to an energetic Irishman from Bridgeton, New Jersey, whose name was Dick Toben. Toben, an engineer, salesman and superb story teller, came to Simplot with some experience in food processing of other vegetables. His ideas and ingenuity were basically responsible for the continuous flow stainless steel fryers and the system for cleaning frying fat to prevent waste and rancidity.

Once these technical problems were solved, only the problem of introducing the new product to enough people remained. Distribution and demand grew by leaps and bounds and from those days in the early 1950s, the Simplot food division has rarely been able to keep up with the demand for their frozen French fries and their other frozen products.

In 1946 Simplot bought a processing plant in Burley for the production of dehydrated potato granules and it went into production under the name of the Shelley Processing Company. In 1947 a potato starch plant was purchased in Jerome, Idaho.

In 1960 a new concept in potato utilization became a reality with the construction of the huge Simplot potato processing complex at Heyburn, Idaho, just across the river from Burley. This industrial community included processing lines for various frozen and dehydrated potato products, a potato starch plant, and a modern packing warehouse for fresh potatoes.

The Heyburn concept permitted the Simplot Company to bring field-run potatoes into the area, utilize the cosmetically perfect potatoes for fresh shipments, choose the ideal size and physical characteristics for frozen French fries and other frozen products, manufacture dehydrated potato products from the smaller sizes and send the balance to the starch plant for the extraction and modification of potato starch. The economics of such an operation were favorable since a minimum of handling was necessary after the sorting operation took place. The area of conflict proved to be the fresh shipping operation and the frozen French fry lines. The huge demands of the freezing line left very few potatoes to be shipped fresh, so the fresh packing operations were not utilized on a regular basis.

In addition, quantities of tubers were trucked to the Shelley dehydration plant across the river in Burley. Large storage facilities were built at the Heyburn site for both raw potatoes and frozen products.

As well planned and managed as the system was, it became obsolete with the tremendous growth in the frozen potato industry that took place in the 1975 to 1985 period. Frozen French fries, particularly for the foodservice market, became the dominant product. Becoming a major supplier of frozen French fries for the McDonald's chain of fast food restaurants, and supplying other major chains as well, dictated huge expansion by Simplot in frozen production capacity. Potato wastes were utilized for livestock feed and more recently for the production of ethanol. The economics of supplying the growing French fry market led to the Simplot Company becoming specialized in frozen potato production and discontinuing dehydrated products, an area in which it had been a pioneer.

A growing market for frozen potato products made it necessary for Simplot to increase production capacity. In 1973 plants built by other companies were purchased by Simplot in Crookston, Minnesota, Idaho Falls and Aberdeen, Idaho. In 1977 the company built a frozen processing plant at Hermiston, Oregon, and purchased a processing facility at Grand Forks, North Dakota.

The J. R. Simplot Company participated in the development of the Automatic Defect Removal system, which greatly reduced trim table labor, and in the use of railroad cars refrigerated with liquid carbon dioxide for shipping frozen foods. The company also built a $6 million research and development center at the Caldwell plant site.

In the early 1990s the growth in domestic sales of frozen French fries has slowed. Existing plants are adequate to supply demand. The popularity of pizza restaurants and ethnic foods has slowed the increase in frozen French fry consumption.

To continue growth, the Simplot Company has looked elsewhere. New frozen products including flavored French fries and curly cuts have helped, and more recently frozen mashed potatoes have been introduced.

Considerable development has also been accomplished in the international market with particular emphasis on exports to Asia where processed potatoes are now being accepted along with other western foods. The Simplot food group has its own sales offices in some Asian countries and sells through trading companies in others.

71

The overseas expansion of McDonald's has increased Simplot's export business since a large portion of the potatoes are supplied by the Simplot Company. It is not likely that most Asian countries will grow their own processing potatoes because their land and climate are not suitable.

The Simplot food group has diversified its offerings into other areas of food products--most aimed at the foodservice market.

Although foodservice products comprise the lion's share of Simplot production and marketing, a line of MicroMagic retail items has been created and will be expanded as additional products are developed.

J. R. Simplot presently has three large potato processing plants in Idaho located in Caldwell, Heyburn and Aberdeen. Recently the company has reentered the fresh shipping business with two packing warehouses in Idaho Falls and one in Aberdeen.

The history of J. R. Simplot's potato empire has been one of steady growth with an emphasis on flexibility—the willingness to get into new areas that offer opportunities and likewise abandon enterprises that fail to show growth opportunity or profit. Company policy indicates that the future will be no different with perhaps more of the expansion taking place in the international market.

Chapter VII
IDAHO POTATO SHIPPERS
BECOME "MARKETERS"
FOR INDUSTRY

The establishment, growth and evolution of the potato shipping segment of the industry in Idaho is the history of changing technology and changing methods of merchandising. In the very early days, growers sorted and packed their own crops. The work was usually done in the potato cellar and was primarily a family operation. Grading standards were almost nonexistent and the sorting process was largely to separate smaller potatoes which would be the seed for next year's crop along with clods of dirt, field stones and trash which were completely unacceptable as food.

The early sorting operations were not mechanized. A hand-powered shaker sorter was employed and the potatoes were "dry" packed which meant they were not washed. The person who eventually became a potato shipper evolved through the invention and employment of electrically-powered sorting tables. This early equipment was not very complicated, but it did involve a moving belt on a table which carried the potatoes by people standing on either side and enabled them to remove defective tubers and to make selection according to size if so desired.

When a grower invested his money in a portable sorting table, it was customary to move it from cellar to cellar and work for his neighbors after his own crop had been shipped. It was also customary for the grower who owned a sorting table to have a crew working for him so that he could handle the entire operation, perhaps utilizing the labor of the grower he was working with or a member or two of his family in addition to the regular crew. These growers who sorted and packed potatoes for others tended to become specialists and so developed the evolution of the country shipper.

When it was necessary to use horses as a means of transporting the potatoes to the railroad, hauling distances had to be very short. If a farm was located four or five miles from the town where the potatoes could be loaded on a railroad car, it was usually possible for the teamster to make only two trips per day. As cellars to store potatoes were built along the railroads in Idaho's small towns, it was only natural that sorting facilities would be installed at these potato warehouses so that shipping could continue during the cold months of the winter replacing the family operation in the grower's cellar.

As the Idaho potato industry grew in size, the number of individual people involved in shipping operations also greatly increased. Nampa, Twin Falls, Burley, Aberdeen, Blackfoot, Pocatello, Shelley, Idaho Falls, Rexburg, Rigby and many other Idaho communities had their so-called "spud alley" where potato shipping warehouses had been

Most employees were men in early shipping operations.

Washing potatoes was an early marketing innovation.

built along the railroad.

As the packing function became separated from the growing aspect, the potato shipper became a dealer and began to be a prominent and influential man in the potato industry. The shippers came from three sources. There were the people like Jack Simplot who were first growers and, seeing the opportunities in the shipping industry, established themselves as dealers. There were people like Ed Harper, Sr. who had been in the produce business at the terminal market end and sensed a business opportunity in Idaho as an originator of potato shipments. There were also those in southwest Idaho who had produce sheds already in operation in which they were sorting and packing apples, prunes, pears and other fruit grown in that section of the state. By adding potatoes and onions to their list of commodities, they were able to keep their crews and facilities busy through the winter after the fruit had been handled.

In eastern Idaho, names such as Fielding, Sage, Holland, Christensen and Burnett numbered among the very earliest shipping operations. The Idaho Potato Growers Cooperative was also one of the early shippers of Idaho® potatoes. Ed Harper established his business at Pocatello under the name of Idaho Pack and proved to be one of the leaders and innovative merchandisers of the Idaho potato business. As the number of shippers proliferated, it was estimated that, at the peak, there were more than 200 shipping warehouses in the state buying potatoes from growers and packing them in 100-lb. burlap bags for sale to cash track buyers, jobbers and carlot receivers outside the state with or without the help of brokers.

Lack of grading standards and government inspections left the contents of the potato bags up to the conscience of the dealer who was doing the packing. Ethical considerations were minimal and the quality of merchandise that went into the bag depended a great deal on what was available and the business practices of the shipper involved.

Carloads of potatoes were sold to cash track buyers or it became a common practice for some Idaho shippers to roll their cars unsold. Once under way on the railroad, the shippers would make a call to a potato broker or commission merchant in Chicago who would endeavor to sell the car there or divert it to another receiving point. Under these conditions, the seller and the buyer had no contact with each other and prior to the development of private brands, the buyer had nothing on which to gauge the quality of his purchase until he unloaded the potatoes at the terminal market.

As buyers began opening cars and sampling shipments, a practice known as "stove piping" developed at the shipping point in Idaho. A few good potatoes were put in the bottom of the bag, a stove pipe was then inserted in the center section and good potatoes packed around the stove pipe. The space inside the stove pipe was then filled with small potatoes, culls and a conglomerate of off-grade merchandise that would probably cause the buyer to turn down the shipment if he knew it was present. The pipe was then withdrawn from the burlap bag and a few good potatoes packed on top before the bag was sewn shut. When the

Mechanical sizing facilitated uniformity in packages.

Terminal market repacker fills ten-pound bags with Idaho russets.

prospective buyer opened the bag from the top he was greeted by the sight of good potatoes. If he chose to slit the side or the bottom in an attempt to find out what the rest of the bag contained, he also found quality merchandise. But when the entire container was unpacked, it had its share of poor grade potatoes which had been stove piped into the middle of the bag. This practice was perhaps the darkest day in the history of the Idaho shipping industry in customer relations and an appreciation for quality.

Men such as grower-shipper Joe Marshall are given credit for establishing the principle that quality was an important factor in marketing Idaho® potatoes. Marshall took great pride in his crop and insisted it be handled carefully and he put only merchandise of which he was proud in bags bearing his brand. It soon became known that the Joe Marshall Blue Diamond brand commanded a premium price in Chicago, California, Kansas City and points east. It was generally accepted that Marshall's potatoes were worth at least an extra twenty-five cents a hundred sight unseen.

Other shippers soon followed suit when they realized that the introduction of the Russet Burbank had given the state of Idaho a unique product to sell, and quality began to be the watch word of Idaho potato shippers.

Establishing a reputation for quality was not an easy matter for a shipper. Potatoes were purchased from the grower on a "pack out" basis. This meant that potatoes were never weighed as they entered the dealer's packing shed, but were passed over the sorting table and separated into number ones and number twos. The culls were diverted for seed, starch or livestock feed. The grower was then paid on the number of ones and twos that were packed out of his crop and loaded on the railroad car.

Growers were not anxious to sell their crop to the shipper who was extremely fastidious about the quality that went into the bags since this usually meant a lower total dollar return to them. Growers frequently spent the entire time their lots were being sorted in the shipper's warehouse with "their heads in the cull chute" as the dealers described it. As a matter of fact, suspicion was wide spread among growers that dishonest shippers were somehow stealing a portion of each lot of potatoes that they bought from the growers. Not knowing the exact weight of the potatoes they brought to the warehouse, the number of bags loaded on railroad cars always seemed short of the growers' expectations from their crops. Although the farmer had no alternative market for his crop, relations were frequently less than cordial between the man who grew the crop and the dealer who sorted, packed and shipped it.

The 1930s was a period in which the Idaho potato shipping industry established itself. Production had grown to 16,146,000 hundredweight by 1930 and Idaho® potatoes were gaining their national reputation for baking quality and the higher grading standards of Idaho shippers. With the expansion of potato acreage in Idaho and the increased importance of the Idaho® potato in national markets, sales problems began to develop. Chicago became the potato sales center for the nation and most of the cars of Idaho®

potatoes that left the state were handled or influenced by Chicago potato interests. Idaho growers and shippers found it increasingly difficult to operate at the prices they received as a result of the virtual marketing monopoly of the Chicago group.

Potato growers and shippers in Idaho found a unique solution to their problem. Believing that a demand could be developed for Idaho® potatoes in major cities all over the United States, Idaho industry people caused the Idaho Fruit and Vegetable Advertising Commission to be created by a legislative act. After a "day in court" on which the constitutionality of the advertising concept was challenged, the promotional body set out to make the nation aware of Idaho's uniquely superior product.

A new spirit of working together was born in the shipping industry which performed the marketing function, and a general feeling developed that grading standards must be stricter and Idaho must deliver the superior quality potatoes that its advertising messages promised the American housewife.

Through the trying days of World War II, the Idaho potato industry kept on marketing its products. The shippers had the problem of government priority diverting a substantial portion of the crop into processing channels for military needs. Fresh potatoes for the army and navy were also packed in Idaho in wooden crates—a new and different package for shippers to deal with. What potatoes were available to be shipped fresh were sold readily and the Advertising Commission adapted the sales message to war-

81

Fancy gift packs call for foil wrapping.

One of the early innovative Idaho shippers was Bill Bailey.

time conditions.

During the '40s another change took place in the Idaho shipping industry. Shippers found supplies more difficult to get and their relationships with customers growing stronger. To enable them to supply regular accounts, many of the shippers also got into the growing business. During this period the grower-shipper concept grew from the exception to the common practice. This enabled shippers to provide a more dependable supply of potatoes to their customers since they could ship their own crop when they were not able to buy supplies from growers.

The late '40s saw an upgrading of merchandising practices and the advent of washing potatoes before packing them in Idaho. Once the American housewife had experienced the convenience of buying potatoes in the store from which the field dirt had been removed, she made her preference for washing known. Even though the washing process revealed defects that could not be easily detected in a dry pack and showed some other disadvantages in keeping qualities and shelf life, the practice became virtually universal in the industry.

During this period shippers also began supplying consumer size units. The market share of national supermarket chains was growing, and the traditional broker-jobber sequence in the market was being by-passed. Chains which were able to buy straight cars of potatoes to be unloaded at their own warehouses, however, preferred consumer-size bags which did not need repacking before they could be put on display in stores. Such giant merchandising organizations as Kroger and A&P actually had their own resident buying organizations in Idaho.

At the same time, preference for Idaho® potatoes in the foodservice field was growing and restaurant operators proved to be quite willing to pay a higher price to get carefully sized and selected potatoes. Not only were Idaho shippers purchasing equipment for packing five and ten-pound consumer bags, they were buying sizing machines which enabled them to pack a closely sized fifty-pound carton which proved to be the most convenient unit for the restaurant operator, a unit which could also be sold to the supermarket for bulk displays of premium quality bakers. Shippers who refused to keep up with the new merchandising and marketing methods found it increasingly difficult to compete, and signs were beginning to appear that the Idaho potato shipping industry was due for some drastic changes.

The '70s and '80s saw many of the old time shippers retire to be replaced by a cadre of young forward-looking people. Many old facilities were abandoned for new modernized plants with greater capacity and improved efficiency. Potato processors were adding fresh shipping departments which were state-of-the-art. However, exclusively fresh warehouses being built, like Bonded Produce, Inc. and Circle Valley Produce, Inc., both in Idaho Falls, were also large-capacity operations with no expense spared in equipment and design.

The demand for cartons and consumer bags of sized potatoes created new problems for shippers. It meant enlargement and remodelling of shipping warehouses and investments in expensive mechanical and electronic sizing equipment. Those operators who had a number of small warehouses simply could not afford to update all of them and there was only enough room in the industry for a limited number of large volume shippers.

With all of its virtues of flavor, texture and keeping qualities, the Russet Burbank variety is difficult to grow and consistently produces a high percentage of U. S. number one tubers. The expanding processing industry in Idaho was utilizing the processor grade (misshapen, undersized and overly large potatoes) that the shippers could not pack, so economics demanded that surviving fresh shippers have a plant within hauling distance to sell that portion of the field-run crop.

Water quality standards became more stringent during this period which meant that the water used in a shipping warehouse to wash potatoes and to transport them in flumes could no longer be dumped in the nearest drain ditch, river or creek without treatment. This factor added another increment of expense that spelled the end of the small shipping shed.

The progressive, aggressive shippers took customers away from those who would not break with the past. The Simplot Produce Company, the J. H. Henry Company, the E. S. Harper operation, L. E. Stephens, Bonded Produce, Idaho Potato Growers, T. S. Vanderford, Harvey Schwendiman, Winslow Whiteley, L. S. Taube, Blick and Reese, Rolland Jones Potatoes and Max Herbold were some of the shippers to establish themselves in the new competitive situation with progressive merchandising and a reputation for quality in the brands they packed.

The early '50s saw even greater changes taking place as the processing industry developed. The number of potatoes going into processed products increased and processors needed the same field-run lots of potatoes that shippers had traditionally utilized. Many of the best growers contracted their crops to processors, making them unavailable for fresh market sales. Processing companies were actively bidding for raw supplies which formerly shippers purchased for the fresh market. Some shippers, like Winslow Whiteley, saw the future in processing and ceased shipping operations to join a group that built a frozen French fry plant in Burley.

At the same time, concentration of buying power in the markets was taking place at a rapid rate. In the 1930s a shipper might have a list of 2,500 customers that he could sell to with some regularity. Produce distribution patterns throughout the country included many small jobbers who could buy a car of Idaho® potatoes, unload it at the produce terminal in their city, and sell it to small chains, restaurants and independent grocery outlets.

As supermarket chains became stronger and eliminated their competition, the wholesalers and jobbers began to disappear. This meant that Idaho shippers had fewer customers to sell to and the concentration continued to the point where fifteen of the largest buyers in the country were taking seventy-five to eighty percent of all Idaho® fresh potatoes which were marketed.

When potatoes were nearly all shipped in 100-lb. burlap

bags, they were a true commodity. Sellers and buyers almost never met and middle men in the industry controlled the flow of merchandise. Sizing, the growing quality reputation of Idaho, and a variety of different packs in consumer bags contributed to the need for a more aggressive and specialized type of marketing. Shippers found that they needed to satisfy special needs and cement relations with customers. What had formerly been only a voice on a telephone became a real person at a produce convention or a customer to be called on when making a trade trip. The dealers who adapted, survived; those who did not, went out of business.

At the same time that a rapidly changing market was demanding adaptation in Idaho, potato growers in other parts of the United States were looking enviously at the premium price that Idaho® potatoes commanded. They began experimenting with growing acreages of russet potatoes in their own production areas with varying degrees of success.

In the beginning, Idaho had a virtual exclusive on the Russet Burbank potato, with its fine cooking qualities and reputation for quality, only to find by the early '50s some production was taking place in Maine, Colorado, Michigan, Wisconsin, Washington and Oregon.

With other sources of russet potatoes available, the identification of Idaho grown potatoes became a problem. Much of the crop was still leaving the state in 100-lb. bags which meant that they could be repacked in the market into consumer-size containers or could be sold from bulk displays

87

in retail produce departments. Consumers could not tell whether they were getting Idaho grown russets or those which came from another producing area.

Idaho required that the Idaho trademark seal be included on every container, but with the premium price genuine Idaho® potatoes would bring, the practices of blending and mislabeling were widespread. Some Idaho shippers felt that consumer packages packed in Idaho and labeled as Idaho® potatoes were the answer to the misrepresentation problem.

Another idea that had a great many advocates was that of stamping individual potatoes with the words "Grown In Idaho." To many this seemed like the ideal solution to the problem; however, it proved to be unsolvable from a technical viewpoint. The effort to make stamping work represented an investment in time and effort by many shippers that in the end had to be abandoned.

Another devastating change was yet to affect the shipping industry. As processing firms grew larger and more influential and controlled more of the production of potatoes in Idaho, the dehydrators in particular found it to their advantage to get into the fresh shipping business as well. The Simplot company had a large fresh shipping business before starting its processing plants, but with most processors, the converse was true. For example the R. T. French Company, of mustard fame, installed a fresh shipping department to compliment their instant mashed potato processing operation at Shelley. Both were later sold to the Pillsbury Co. Sunspiced division of Basic Vegetable Corporation in Blackfoot also found the fresh shipping business advantageous to their dehydration operation.

Conversely, shippers invested in processing plants to round out their operations, such as Rolland Jones Potatoes in Rupert who built a flake plant in 1966 and another in 1985. Idaho Potato Packers in Blackfoot, Idaho Fresh Pak, Inc. in Lewisville, Larsen of Idaho in Hamer, Idaho Supreme Potatoes in Firth and Sun Glo of Idaho in Rexburg are all processors who also ship fresh potatoes. Each year the potato acreage in Idaho became larger, the processing industry's requirements grew, individual fresh shippers did more business, but they became fewer in number.

By the mid-1970s the trends of more processing activity and a shrinking supply for the fresh market had stabilized somewhat. By the early '90s both segments of the industry are larger than ever and seem to be permanent partners in the Idaho potato industry. Idaho growers, shippers and processors all have good reasons for wanting to stay in the business of supplying fresh potatoes to consumers and the foodservice industry.

The shippers that have survived have in a large part become more marketing and merchandising oriented and potatoes in both fresh and processed forms seem to be an integral and permanent part of the American diet. Pacific rim markets have also been introduced to processed Idaho® potatoes and the export potential is huge if the acceptance of Western food continues to increase. It would be difficult to pay tribute to all of the people who were responsible for growth, innovation and changes in the Idaho shipping industry. The Idaho Grower Shippers Association did much to hold the industry together and to pursue the common goals of its members.

Edd Moore, who served as executive manager of the association through the '50s and '60s, kept the organization's attention focused on problems as they developed and provided solutions whenever possible. Upon Moore's retirement in 1973, Meldon B. Anderson took over the organization's reins and served until 1980 when he left to accept the executive manager's job at Potato Growers of Idaho. Anderson was ably replaced by Dave Smith who in the early '90s still guides the organization's activities.

IGSA has interested itself in the industry's transportation problems and marketing practices and, through the efforts of the capable executive managers, directors and various committees, accomplished much in upgrading Idaho shipping practices which helped establish the Idaho® potato as the number one produce commodity in the nation.

Chapter VIII
"RUSSET" PROMOTED TO INTERNATIONAL FAVORITE BY IDAHO POTATO COMMISSION

The Idaho Fruit and Vegetable Advertising Commission, the first official body to advertise fruits and vegetables from the Gem state, was created by the 1937 Idaho Legislature. It held its organizational meeting May 10, 1937, and the new law included potatoes, onions, apples and prunes in the group of crops to be promoted.

Two weeks later by majority vote of the Idaho Fruit and Vegetable Advertising Commission members, Cline Advertising Service of Boise (no longer in business) and Botsford, Constantine and Gardner of Portland (now Ketchum Communications in San Francisco) were named as advertising agents. These two firms serviced and maintained the account until 1973 when Foote, Cone & Belding of San Francisco was selected to replace Ketchum.

The newly created Commission immediately embarked on a campaign to promote Idaho produce in newspapers, radio and magazines throughout the country. The first advertising budget for russets included $19,052 for newspaper ads and $2,612 for radio. Money to finance the program was to come from tax assessment of one cent per hundredweight paid entirely by the growers.

The first year, Idaho russet potatoes were advertised in fifty-three newspapers and on radio in ten cities. In August of 1937, $1,000 was authorized for advertising in *Restaurant Management* magazine and $250 for menu tip-ons. An educational program on the proper handling and treatment of potatoes was implemented in the state of Idaho.

The promotion of the Idaho® potato was launched!

July 27, 1937, saw the first dealer service man, Lloyd Bell, approved by the Commission for work in California. With the steady growth of the industry and Commission programs, the field merchandising activity has continued to grow in manpower and importance through the years.

The newspaper space budget had grown to $58,174 by 1938 and was $51,743 in 1939.

In the middle of that second year, one of the first major actions to provide a uniform label that could be promoted for the Idaho potato industry was undertaken. The advertising commission suggested a uniform bag design with the purpose of identifying Idaho® potatoes The regulations specified colored stripes on bags and packages denoting grade of potatoes (number ones, number twos, or combinations) and a new logotype design "Idaho" to be appropriately displayed.

In 1938 an experimental plant to produce alcohol from potatoes was being constructed in Idaho Falls under the direction of the University of Idaho, and the Advertising Commission was persuaded to contribute $3,000 to the project.

In spite of early successes, not everyone in the industry favored paying a tax to finance promotion of Idaho commodities and the Commission found itself involved in heated discussions and legal action concerning its right to levy an advertising tax on fruits and vegetables. A friendly lawsuit was undertaken which established the legality of the statute, but it was still necessary to change the law to quiet unrest in the industry. The 1939 Legislature eliminated apples and prunes from the program, changed the name to the Idaho Advertising Commission and cut the advertising tax on potatoes and onions from one cent to one-half cent per hundredweight. Also seed potatoes were exempt from the tax.

Under the lower tax rate, advertising in newspapers was budgeted at $21,500 in 1940 and 1941, but dropped lower to $16,000 in 1942 and 1943, the early war years. As production increased in the industry, the next few years saw a steady increase and by 1947 the newspaper budget was $42,825.

At several meetings in 1947 the Commission discussed placing a seal on every bag of Idaho® potatoes to prevent receivers from "stripping" the bakers from the bags, refilling with small-sized and overly large potatoes and re-sewing the containers shut.

Although the amount of the tax was deducted from the payment to the grower by the first handler (shipper or processor), the shippers were responsible for payment to the Commission. Delinquent tax payments proved to be a

Members
Idaho Advertising Commission
1940

E. N. Pettygrove
Commissioner of
Agriculture, Chairman

Chas. W. Barlow
Hazelton

L.L. Hurst
Caldwell

Joe Marshall
Twin Falls

Members
Idaho Advertising Commission
1940

H. G. Peckham
Wilder

Frank Westfall
Aberdeen

E. A. White
Lewiston

William Wulf
Idaho Falls

constant problem from the very beginning of the program.

During this era about half of the potato harvesting was done by school children who were granted a special "spud vacation" to work in the fields. In 1947 they earned an estimated $800,000 for their work. But as the industry grew, the need for more farm laborers was apparent and the Commission's agencies did extensive advertising in the southwest section of the United States to encourage Mexican laborers to help in Idaho's fields.

A legal agreement was entered into by the state of Idaho, acting by and through the Idaho Agricultural Experimental Station for the University of Idaho, to conduct research activities with regard to mechanical harvesting of potatoes and reducing potato losses. This agreement was legalized in 1948 starting a long and profitable relationship between the University and the Commission, still in existence today.

Two popular items created to advertise Idaho® potatoes were toothpick flags placed in bakers by restaurants and consumer recipe folders. Both items were used in huge quantities. The most memorable was a premium offer of a thirty-cent French fry cutter. The Commission's initial manufacture order was for 10,000 cutters in June, 1948. The first promotion was in November and by December, 19,000 requests for the kitchen devices had been received at the Commission office. Three months later 28,524 requests had been received.

The French fry cutters were so successful the Commission decided to "go it again" during the fiscal year

1949-50 and 32,500 cutters were sent as premiums. But, of the total, almost 10,000 had to be replaced by the manufacturers because of weak wires. Many cards and letters were sent by housewives complaining of breakage, and finally, a cutter was devised that would withstand two hundred pounds of pressure.

In December, 1951, the threat of price ceilings was a grave concern to the Commission as Idaho® potatoes were bringing well over $1 per hundredweight more than potatoes from other producing areas. A committee was set up to coordinate the efforts of Idaho's fight against price ceilings and was comprised of representatives of the Advertising Commission, the Producer's Association, Cooperatives, the Idaho State Grange, Idaho Farm Bureau, the shippers and the Idaho Potato Industry Coordinating Committee. C. G. Rice, the dealer service man at the time, was sent to Washington, D. C., so he would be available to do what was necessary to fight price ceilings. This issue concerned the Commission until about the middle of 1952 when price ceilings were rolled back.

In 1952 consumer advertising, including space and production, was budgeted at $80,000 and increased $10,000 to $90,000 in 1953. The total advertising budget was $165,000 in 1954 and the consumer advertising portion was $95,000.

With the quality reputation of Idaho® potatoes being established nation wide a major problem facing the industry in the mid-1950s was how to identify the product as being GROWN in Idaho. Potatoes grown in other states were "riding" on the Commission's promotions and making claims to be "like Idahos" or being repacked in Idaho bags to profit from the premium price commanded by Idaho grown potatoes.

In the summer of 1955, application for the "Grown in Idaho" trademark was filed in the U. S. Patent Office. The trademark was used on bags and boxes of potatoes leaving Idaho, but they sometimes ended up by being repacked with russets not grown in the Gem State. The ideal solution seemed to be to identify each and every potato that deserved the premium price.

A determined effort taken by the Commission was a program to stamp "Grown In Idaho" on every number one potato. This resulted in the need for some sort of stamping machine. Commission members were so certain that the stamping machine was the answer that they supported the program strongly. Shippers were also convinced that this type of identification was necessary and many bought stamping machines and began operating them in their warehouses.

But the problems occurring with the manufacture and operation of such a machine were paramount. Nonuniform stamping, potato deterioration from stamping processes, high costs of purchasing and operating the machines, the threat of a dwindling fresh market and a booming processed market, along with the discovery that housewives really did not want stamped potatoes, killed the stamping machine idea. Finally in 1974 (almost 20 years later) they had to give up on the project.

Potato processor J. R. Simplot appeared in 1956 before the Commission to recommend that advertising tie-ins should include the processing industry. He foresaw a big future for processed potatoes in Idaho and stressed the need for additional research on processed products and methods.

A Commission tally indicated that in December 1957 nine companies in Idaho were processing twenty-eight Idaho® potato products. Four of those companies handled frozen French fries. Dehydrated diced and frozen diced potatoes were processed by five companies. Other items included frozen patties, frozen hash browns, tater rounds, potato flour and frozen crinkle cuts.

Later that year an advertising agency report to the Commission indicated the impact that "millions of newspaper advertisements" had made since the start of the potato promotional program. They showed samples, quantities and costs of sales promotion material used to date, including restaurant potato flags and menu tip-ons, recipe folders, display material and trade broadsides.

John Greenlee, the President of Cline/Inc., presented charts showing by year the values of Idaho® potatoes produced annually since 1937, when it was $7,312,000, to 1954-55, when it was $45,288,000. The peak was $64,170,000 in 1953. He also reported the increased unloads in markets where advertising had been used, and reported that since 1937 the U.S. per capita consumption of Idaho® potatoes had increased 14% while the consumption of all white potatoes had declined 16%.

Contracts with out-of-state repackers for the use of the

Potato stamping machine in use in fresh packing warehouse.

Stamping was considered the answer to the identification problem.

"Grown In Idaho" registration marks were in force in 1956 which enabled the Commission to better track the use and abuse of the Idaho name as a marketing tool.

The year 1957 saw Clyde Domeny join C.G. Rice and Dean Probert to become the third full-time dealer service man working major U.S. food markets . That same year the Legislature passed a bill allowing the name Idaho Potato and Onion Commission to replace Idaho Advertising Commission.

One of many trademark violations occurred in 1958 when a Canadian shipping firm began advertising russet potatoes as "Idaho Type Russets," and the Commission concluded that not only did the Idaho® potato need to be identified as being grown in Idaho, it needed to be identified as to where it was packed.

The end of Lee Heller's career with the IP&OC, after 12 years as Commission secretary, came with his resignation in 1958. He was replaced by Gerald A. Lee.

Later, in 1959, a Commission regulation was directed to all companies making bags for Idaho® potatoes: all Idaho® potatoes   packaged for human consumption are to be identified with the "Grown In Idaho" trademark and also "Packed in Idaho by . . . ." is to be imprinted on the bag in appropriate sized type.

Consumer advertising amounted to $315,000 during the 1960-1961 year. Also in 1960, an extension potato marketing project was begun to provide leadership for potato marketing education within the state.

In 1961 one of the major changes in the Commission

took place. Until that time the law placed no limit on the amount of time a commissioner could serve. Several of the members had been on the body a decade or more. With the growing importance of the potato processing industry within the state, processors began to want representation on the Commission, but at that time no legal machinery existed for appointing a representative from the processing industry. The result was the submission of House Bill #238 to the Idaho Legislature which incorporated some sweeping changes.

Besides those factions that wanted change, there was also strong support for keeping the Commission as it was and the bill became controversial. Late at night, within an hour of adjournment, the bill was brought out on the floor and passed and in mid-March Governor Robert E. Smylie signed the measure into law. At the July meeting the new nine-member body was seated for the first time.

Commissioners were now limited to two three-year terms and the membership was increased from six to nine. The law stipulated that two members must be potato processors, two potato shippers and five must be growers. The days of entrenched members were gone forever.

Another provision of the new law, known as the Piper amendment, required that any appropriation of money from the 12 1/2% of IP&OC funds earmarked for research and grower education must be passed by six or more affirmative votes.

Another decision made that year was the launching of a monthly publication, the *Idaho Potato and Onion News,* and the hiring of Jay Sherlock to be editor. Sherlock was later to become Executive Secretary of the Commission.

The highlights of 1961, as enumerated by the Commission's executive secretary, were the decision to publish the *Idaho Potato and Onion News*, the initiation of monthly auditing and billing to keep tax payments current, and the study of the possibility of developing a multi-wall paper container for 100 pound units.

Gradually the Commission office procedure was becoming more efficient and up-to-date when the new billing system went into effect in 1961 and a method was devised for keeping records on processor grade potatoes being sold by first handlers to processors. The problem of collecting delinquent advertising tax was constant.

A summary of twenty-six states and the District of Columbia showed that publication space amounting to $62,000 in value was obtained in publicity and tie-ins in the 1962-63 financial year.

Work on a state-of-the-art research laboratory at the University's Aberdeen Experiment Station was started later in 1963. The IP&OC contributed $118,000 of the $315,117 total cost of the project and encouraged the University to name the facility the Joe Marshall Potato Research Center. The center provides approximately 12,000 square feet of laboratory and controlled storage space. The research center is directed by the Idaho Agricultural Experiment Station with all work conducted in cooperation with Idaho's potato industry and the Agricultural Research Service of USDA.

Early in 1964 one of the Commissioners attending the United Fresh Fruit and Vegetable Association convention reported back that the Idaho potato booth "stole the show."

By the middle of the year, C.G. Rice had worked twenty-five years as a fieldman for the Commission. He was credited with being with the Commission continually longer than any other person at that time.

The beginning of the direct involvement of the IP&OC with transportation problems began the middle of 1964, when it was suggested that a fund be established to hire a rate expert. The fund was to be financed by the various Idaho commissions such as wheat, bean and prune.

Talk of potato calories was heard at Commission meetings toward the end of 1965, and efforts to counteract the "potatoes are fattening" publicity were made.

In February of 1965 Gerald A. Lee submitted his resignation to the Commission, stating that he had accepted a position with the Department of Agriculture in Hawaii. Jay Sherlock, who had been publishing the *Idaho Potato and Onion News* , was one of the many who applied for the job of executive secretary and was subsequently hired after the search committee had screened the applicants.

In December of that year it was announced that Idaho® potatoes would be advertised on national television for the first time on The Today Show and The Tonight Show. At this time it was estimated that, even with the successful marketing of the large 1963 crop, the Idaho potato industry had been able to put only one ten-pound bag of potatoes in each two and one-half homes throughout the nation.

A consumer advertising budget of $300,000 for television was appropriated for the 1966-67 season and a national television push for the Idaho® potato was underway. Also during the first of 1966 the point-of-origin labeling bill was drafted by a potato industry executive and legal coordinator.

The midyear meeting of the Commission held a hearing on adopting the registered ® to identify the Idaho® potato. Discussion on what legal protection the trademark "Grown In Idaho" and registration mark ® gave the industry resulted in licensing dealers to use the symbols. A certification mark license agreement was to be signed each year by the shipper or processor and the Commission before the registered mark could be used.

Later in that year 20-second commercials on film were combined with the live commercials used on The Today Show. The experience with that show was so favorable that the advertising was continued until May at an additional cost of $61,000.

The utilization of Idaho's potato crop was obviously changing as demand increased for processed products and growers sold more of their potatoes to processors. Advertising and promotional programs adapted to the change and the Commission's fieldmen started a dual role of representing both fresh and processed potatoes in their contacts.

Mechanical harvesting and handling had increased the losses from bruised potatoes and an anti-bruise campaign was initiated to educate growers and handlers how to minimize bruising and surface cuts. An in-state campaign

106

proclaimed "Bruisers Are Losers" using newspapers, radio, equipment stickers and posters.

The campaign to counteract the idea that potatoes are fattening was gaining ground and it was noted that one national magazine published a diet featuring potatoes on the menu every day.

The subject of repackers' agreements was discussed thoroughly early in 1968, as the Commission members realized that the protection of the trademark and registered ® were of prime importance.

In April, 1966, the IP&OC combined promotional programs with the Idaho Eastern-Oregon Onion Committee and the following year, 1967, onions left the Idaho Commission and it became the Idaho Potato Commission. The similarities in the eastern Oregon and Idaho onions made a combined advertising campaign advantageous to the producers in both states.

Later in the year an inventory report of eighty-one Idaho shippers indicated that 4,788,752 consumer units, 269,406 burlap bags, 129,206 paper masters and 50-pound bulks and 11,961 cartons were in stock. All containers by this time were required to carry the official Idaho trademark. Advertising was used to stress the fact that only potatoes grown in Idaho could carry the Idaho trademark.

The only exception was the somewhat gray area of Malheur County which was advertising Idaho-Oregon potatoes using the combined names. This operation involved potatoes grown in Idaho and processed in Oregon and vice versa.

Commissioners participating in the Japan Food Fair in 1969 brought home ideas of exploring the overseas markets. They stressed that stimulation of the Japan market toward potato use would be a distinct advantage for the Idaho processing business. Western influences were very noticeable in Japan and a new food might very well interest the Japanese housewife.

In November of 1969 it was suggested that the Idaho Potato Commission evaluate the practice of shipping potatoes out of the state in bulk lots. This issue was very hotly contested between growers and shippers as many growers favored it, but most shippers saw it as a threat to their businesses. The discussions continued as the executive secretary of the Idaho Grower Shippers Association said Idaho shippers were worried that they would lose all identity protection.

Statistics were quoted by the IGSA showing the decline of one-hundred pound bags of fresh potatoes. The 1966 crop had fifty-seven percent of all fresh potatoes shipped in one-hundred pound units, whereas the 1967 crop was fifty percent and in1968 only forty-three percent was shipped this way. Fifty-pound count cartons were much in demand and were rapidly replacing the one-hundred pound units.

Another issue that year was an effort to improve quality, to "produce the premium potatoes that we advertise and promote." The industry research and education committee was charged with the responsibility of upgrading the quality of the Idaho® potato.

108

Traffic at the Idaho potato booth at the American Food Service Convention in 1970 was so heavy that it caused congestion problems on the convention floor.

The possibilities of a substantial export business attracted the attention of Commission members in 1970 when they received information from the Foreign Agricultural Service indicating that crops of potatoes were short in Sweden, Denmark, England, Poland, France, and presumably in most other European countries.

In April the Union Pacific Railroad made several tests comparing the conditioned-air bulk cars with refrigerated service (ice bunker) cars. One demonstration involved a car loaded in Boise on April 3 and unloaded in Boston on April 20. A USDA agricultural inspector from Boise supervised the unloading in Boston and evaluated the quality as "okay" and approved the new shipping method.

The gray area in Malheur County, Oregon, was developing into a deep concern to Commission members in 1970 and they were anxious to clarify the questions of whether Oregon had the right to use "Idaho" in their promotional material.

Tensions among staff members surfaced during 1970 and efforts to resolve the problem failed, resulting in the Commission requesting resignations from executive secretary Jay Sherlock and field auditor Reed Huntsman. Sherlock refused the resignation offer and, when his employment was terminated, there was a flurry of media attention across the state. A special committee was named and began the search for a replacement.

109

Pollution awareness was growing across the nation in 1970 and the potato industry instituted research programs concerning waste water disposal at processing and shipping plants, and growers became conscious of irrigation run-off water from potato fields as a possible problem area.

A new policy was adopted in 1971 of having Commission members covering markets with the field merchandisers. Reports came back to the industry that these visits were very enlightening. Special emphasis was placed on the fieldmen as they worked closely with the advertising agencies and the Commission on planning their itineraries. The activities of the fieldmen emphasized that the IPC had developed a coordinated marketing program.

In January of 1971 the executive secretary vacancy was filled with the employment of Frank Floyd who left a sales department job at Rogers Brothers, an eastern Idaho potato processing and fresh shipping firm. Floyd's tenure was to be short, however, and ended when he submitted his resignation in August of 1972.

Two vacancies occurred in the dealer service staff during 1971. In June, Chuck McDaniel resigned to enter the produce brokerage business in Indiana. Dean Probert's colorful 17-year service to the Idaho® potato industry ended with his death following a prolonged illness. Former Idaho Commissioner of Agriculture Robert Reichert was hired to represent Idaho in the eastern United States and Milt Maclin, a merchandising executive with the Florida Citrus Commission, took over the south and southwest territory.

A promotional highlight of 1971 was a nation-wide Idaho® potato retail display contest in which a Ford Pinto automobile was awarded as first prize. The contest produced a record number of entries.

In an effort to become more involved with the people it represented, the Commission developed a program whereby the advertising agencies made their presentations in several Idaho cities before interested industry people. This was to better acquaint the growers, processors and shippers with what the Commission was attempting to do.

A comment heard at a 1971 convention by a Commission member was, "If there was one potato better than an Idaho, God must have kept it for himself." The reputation of the Idaho® potato was flourishing!

During that fall the anti-bruise efforts were showing results. The theme was a bruise-free harvest and schools were set up in a potato quality program. One big help was the broadcasting of predicted soil temperatures on radio stations to warn growers of excessively cold conditions that would cause bruising.

The next year the Idaho potato industry took significant steps to promote export business for Idaho's number-one product and created, with Washington and Oregon, the Tri-State Potato Export Committee. Fresh potatoes couldn't be shipped into Japan because of restrictions, but some Idaho processors were already involved in a substantial volume of export business.

The Japanese diet appeared to be changing and they became interested in dehydrated potato products. They expressed a desire to know more about dehydrators and Idaho sent a processing technician to assist them. He returned to the Commission telling them that "the potential export market is tremendous for frozen French fries throughout the Orient. But it would take an educational program along with the marketing to create the demand."

A suggestion that late blight in potatoes could be a cause of birth defects impelled the Commission to give $7,000 for a joint research program with St. Luke's Presbyterian Hospital in Chicago. Concurrently they appropriated expenditures up to $16,000 to establish research facilities in Idaho for the same purpose.

After a four-month search and screening process Gordon Randall of Boise was hired by the IPC to a redefined position, now called executive director. He had held several executive positions with Boise Cascade Corporation and convinced the Commission that the job should involve more leadership and decision-making authority.

In January of 1973 Edd Moore announced his retirement from the executive manager's job at Idaho Grower Shippers Assn. He had been a regular attender of IPC meetings and often brought developing problems to the attention of the body. His replacement was Meldon B. Anderson, beginning at this point a potato industry career that would lead eventually to the chair of the IPC executive director.

During 1973 Gordon Randall began attending hearings on the state's standards for pollution control. In the latter part of 1973 a proposal was made to obtain Agricultural

Research personnel for a tri-state potato breeding program. Idaho, Oregon and Washington all assumed a part in the program financed largely by the U. S. Department of Agriculture.

An advertising agency review in February of 1973 resulted in the IPC account being awarded to the San Francisco office of Foote Cone & Belding replacing Botsford Ketchum, the agency that had formulated Idaho's promotional programs for 36 years. Cline, Inc., part of the original agency team, was retained in an in-state public relations capacity. Since Foote Cone had no national public relations department, the IPC named Dudley-Anderson Yutzy of New York to carry out publicity and consumer education programs.

The oil embargo and energy crisis brought a host of new problems for IPC consideration in 1973 including freight rate increases that heavily impacted shippers and processors.

Commission members decided in 1974 to turn over the promotional efforts for the Idaho® potato in Japan to the National Potato Promotions Board. The transfer was made in Japan with an Idaho industry representative present to assure the Japanese that Idaho was still very concerned about the market and would be active in the Potato Board's decisions.

One of the important turning points in the activities of the Idaho Potato Commission occurred in 1974 when the Idaho Legislature passed a bill authorizing the Commission to increase the advertising assessment from 2 and 1/4¢ per cwt to a maximum of 4¢ per cwt. For the first time the opportunity to beef up a seriously underfunded advertising program existed. The legislation was the result of an effort supported by the growing, shipping and processing segments of the industry and orchestrated by IPC's executive director.

As Idaho's aggressive programs made competition more difficult for other production areas, their frustration became apparent, and the Washington Potato Commission, early in 1975, began advertising that "Idaho potatoes grow better in Washington," a clear infringement of the "Idaho® potatoes" registered certification mark.

When the content of the Washington ads was brought to the attention of the Idaho Potato Commission by its advertising counsel, the body voted to take whatever legal steps were necessary to stop the practice. Cease and desist letters from the Commission's legal counsel failed to stop the practice, so at their March meeting the IPC voted to instigate a lawsuit naming the members of the Washington Potato Commission and Pacific National Advertising Agency as defendants, asking for damages and a court order to stop the illegal practice.

Washington's attorneys argued that Idaho had abandoned the trademark and that they were within their rights to use Idaho® potatoes as a generic term. The legal process went slowly forward for more than a year and was finally resolved with a decision from the United States Court, District of Idaho.

The judge awarded no monetary damages, but the Washington Commissioners were required to sign a stipulation that the Idaho certification mark was valid and they were "enjoined and restricted from advertising, promoting or holding out to the public potatoes not grown in Idaho as Idaho® potatoes."

There is no doubt that had Idaho ignored the illegal Washington campaign, or if the court had not decided in Idaho's favor, the Idaho name and trademark would have been up for grabs by anyone who wanted to misrepresent a product. The lawsuit attracted national attention and is, in retrospect, one of the most important legal actions that the IPC ever undertook on behalf of the industry.

This case, unfortunately, was not the last misuse of the Idaho trademark, but it did establish with the IPC the necessity to investigate every violation and pursue the instigators, with court action when necessary, to protect the mark.

Packing other potatoes in packages identifying them as Idaho® potatoes is the most common type of violation and a year has not gone by without several cases of this type being brought to the attention of the IPC.

Even Canadian packers have seemingly discovered the profitability of using the Idaho name. Protecting the trademarks seems destined to be a never-ending activity for the Idaho Potato Commission.

As more acres of land were brought into potato production and the promotional job grew, the IPC periodically increased the tax rate to provide more money to keep up with rapidly increasing costs of television and other advertising media. In 1975 the tax rate was set at 3¢

per cwt and in 1976 it was 3.25¢. In September of 1981 the tax was increased to 5¢ per cwt to fund a budget of $3,113,325. By 1988 the budget had grown to $4,941,300 and the assessment rate to 7¢, and $6,464,500 by 1990 at an 8¢ level of tax.

By 1982 the impact of the growing snack food fad was beginning to be felt by the Idaho potato industry. Dehydrated potato flakes were being used as the basic ingredient in Proctor & Gamble's Pringles and dozens of other snack food products. The value of the Idaho trademark seal received new recognition when P & G announced they would use it on their red package of Pringles.

A significant addition to the Commission's staff and function came about in 1984 when Barbara Bertelli was hired as foodservice director to work with the eating-away-from-home industry in the promotion of processed and fresh Idaho® potatoes.

In July of 1987 the announcement of executive director Gordon Randall's retirement ended his 15-year period of service to the Idaho Potato Commission, a time during which the organization made significant gains in stature and achievement. His state of health had long been in decline as the result of a chronic and incurable ailment.

After a thorough search for a replacement, Mel B. Anderson was hired in December of 1987 to be the Commission's executive director. Anderson had been executive manager of the Idaho Grower Shippers Assn. and then executive director of Potato Growers of Idaho, the position he left to take the IPC job.

116

The year 1989 began a three-year period of rapid change for the IPC. Three of the market relations directors in the field; Milt Maclin, Dick Rath and Frieda Poulos retired to be replaced by Larry Whiteside, Don Luchka and Jim Grimm. Barbara Bertelli also left and Don Odiorne was hired as vice president for foodservice and Jack Hansen as vice president for retail merchandising. Sharyl Strongman was added to the staff as foodservice specialist and later promoted to foodservice market relations director.

The Anderson Rothstein advertising agency in San Francisco was hired to handle foodservice advertising and DDB Needham was replaced in the consumer advertising sector by Young and Rubicam. Oglivy Mather, the New York public relations agency that had purchased DAY, was replaced by Creamer, Dickson & Basford to carry out the national P.R. and consumer education programs.

William White replaced Don Luchka on the field staff and William Savilonis, Jr. went to work as the fifth field person.

During the period, the IPC budget continued to increase and the IPC offices were moved to new quarters at 6th and Bannock in Boise. The IPC, in concert with the potato industry and Department of Agriculture, developed a crisis management program and the machinery was set in motion to obtain registration of the Idaho® potato trademark in several foreign countries. Following up on trademark violations remained an important activity.

This period of change and growth, planned by the Idaho Potato Commission, was to assist the industry in the

The Idaho Potato Commission, 1992: Left to right, standing;
Executive Director Mel Anderson, Howard Phillips, William
Loughmiller, Wayne Thiessen, Ray Cammack, Michael Cranney.
Left to right, front row: Don Dixon, Orville Hartman, Jack Parks
and chairman, LaVerelle Stecklein.

promotion and marketing of larger crops of "Famous Idaho®️ potatoes" in an environment of ever-increasing competition.

MEMBERS: IDAHO FRUIT AND VEGETABLE ADVERTISING COMMISSION, IDAHO ADVERTISING COMMISSION, IDAHO POTATO AND ONION COMMISSION, IDAHO POTATO COMMISSION

	From	To
Harry E. Young, Idaho Falls	3/37	7/39
L. R. Halverson, Blackfoot	3/37	7/39
Victor Smith, Burley	3/37	7/39
Joe P. Marshall, Twin Falls	3/37	12/58
George Ames, Emmett	3/37	7/39
R. H. Young, Sr., Parma	3/37	1/39
E. A. White, Lewiston	3/37	5/40
H. G. Peckham, Wilder	1/39	7/55
Frank L. Westfall, Aberdeen	7/39	7/61
L. L. Hurst, Caldwell	7/39	7/41
Charles W. Barlow, Hazelton	7/39	3/46
William Wulf, Idaho Falls	7/39	7/41
I. J. Longteig, Nez Perce	5/40	7/49
Lem Cook, Idaho Falls	7/41	7/49
Henry M. Chase, Nampa	7/41	7/49
Roy Marquess, Burley	3/46	7/47
George Weitz, Caldwell	7/46	7/49
John Snow, Burley	7/47	7/51
Henry Baune, Nez Perce	6/49	3/52

119

N. E. George, Homedale	7/49	7/51
Harvey Schwendiman, Newdale	7/49	7/64
B. J. Moore, Caldwell	7/51	7/61
Merwin Harding, Jr., Nez Perce	3/52	1/53
W. B. Whiteley, Oakley	7/51	7/66
Ralph Kennedy, Nez Perce	1/53	7/55
Oliver Ruen, Clark Fork	7/55	7/61
R. H. Young, Jr., Parma	7/55	7/66
C. J. Marshall, Jerome	12/58	7/65
Cecil Kent, Caldwell	7/51	7/61
Norbert Brinkmann, Idaho Falls	7/61	7/67
Russell Burkman, Idaho Falls	7/61	7/62
E. J. Morgan, Murtaugh	7/61	7/66
Philip E. Batt, Wilder	7/61	7/66
Roy F. Roberts, Blackfoot	7/61	7/65
R. S. Farish, Caldwell	7/61	7/64
Darwin L. Young, Blackfoot	7/62	7/68
Leo Christensen, Shelley	7/64	3/65
Robert Archibald, Idaho Falls	3/65	7/67
Albert Carlsen, Blackfoot	7/65	3/67
Jack Allred, Murtaugh	7/66	7/72
Ronald Ball, Lewisville	7/67	7/73
Rolland Jones, Rupert	7/65	7/71
Luther Roberts, Weiser	7/66	7/69
Donald Robertson, Burley	7/64	7/70
Joe Taylor, Paul	7/66	7/72
William Webster, Rexburg	7/67	7/73
Riley Westergard, Idaho Falls	3/67	7/71
T. Kendell Thornley, Aberdeen	7/68	7/70

Robert S. Skyles, Nampa	7/69	7/75
Robert L. Mercer, Shelley	7/70	10/72
Leonard Schritter, Aberdeen	7/70	7/77
J. Wray Connolly, Boise	7/71	7/73
James W. Henry, Kimberly	7/71	11/75
Clarence A. Parr, Burley	7/72	7/78
Melvin J. West, Paul	7/72	7/78
Richard A. Bissing, Blackfoot	10/72	5/74
Hugo DalSoglio, Burley	8/73	7/80
Lyle Taylor, Lewisville	7/73	7/79
Dell Raybould, Rexburg	7/73	7/79
Bill D. Robinson, Shelley	5/74	9/80
R. L. Stimpson, Nampa	7/75	7/81
G. L. Christensen, Blackfoot	12/75	7/83
Tom McLain, Buhl	7/78	7/84
Darwin Neibaur, Paul	7/78	7/84
Warren Walters, Newdale	7/79	9/85
Gary Ball, Rexburg	7/79	9/85
Albert M. Johnson, Pocatello	7/79	7/83
John Catey, Boise	7/80	9/86
Roger Jones, Rupert	9/80	9/88
Allen Wood, Caldwell	7/81	1/86
Fred Thompson, Shelley	7/83	9/89
Russ Wynn, American Falls	7/83	9/89
Don Wolverton, Murtaugh	7/84	9/90
Perry Gillette, Paul	7/84	9/90
LeRoy Reed, Idaho Falls	9/85	9/91
John Stanger, Idaho Falls	9/85	9/88
Dave Clapier, Marsing	1/86	9/90

Bill Daniels, Boise	9/86	11/90
Ray Cammack, Idaho Falls	9/88	PS*
Jack Parks, Blackfoot	9/88	PS*
Howard Phillips, Blackfoot	9/89	PS*
LaVerelle Stecklein, Blackfoot	9/89	PS*
Mike Cranney, Oakley	9/90	PS*
Orville Hartman, Parma	9/90	PS*
Bill Loughmiller, Twin Falls	9/90	PS*
Wayne Thiessen, Boise	11/90	PS*
Don Dixon, Idaho Falls	9/91	PS*

* Presently serving

COMMISSION SECRETARIES, EXECUTIVE SECRETARIES AND EXECUTIVE DIRECTORS

Carl L. DeLong	1937
L. E. Sargent	1939
E. N. Pettygrove	1944
L. S. Heller	1946
Gerald A. Lee	1958
Jay R. Sherlock	1965
Frank Floyd	1971
Gordon C. Randall	1972
Mel B. Anderson	1987

Chapter IX
ADVERTISING AND
PR AGENCIES
COURT CONSUMERS, FOODSERVICE

Americans have a love-hate relationship with advertising, and so do clients to some degree with advertising agencies. While many people find some advertising irritating, some boring, almost everyone finds certain of the creative work in ads to be pleasing, humorous and even beautiful.

In this atmosphere it is unusual for client-agency relationships to exist for long periods of time. Accounts are acquired and lost and employees hired and fired in an endless game of musical chairs.

The first 36 years of the Idaho Potato Commission's agency relationship were a notable exception to the common practice of clients changing agencies every five years. When the original agency competition was held, firms from all over the U. S. made presentations. The winner was a combination of two agencies; Botsford, Constantine and Gardner of Portland, Oregon, and Cline Advertising Service of Boise, Idaho.

The combination provided the extensive financial and creative resources of a "big city" agency with the convenience and day-to-day service of a local office located only a few blocks from the client. In the first few years of the relationship other Idaho agencies demanded that, since the Commission was a state agency, they should have "a chance at the account." Two agency reviews actually took place, but the Botsford-Cline group were successful in retaining the business.

Two men, Dave Botsford of the Portland office and John Greenlee of Cline, were largely responsible for charting an efficient and effective strategy for the Idaho potato industry. The Commission was well justified in maintaining the relationship on the basis of sales results in the market place and the rapid growth of Idaho potato awareness in every corner of the nation. The agencies did a remarkable job of getting the maximum results from every dollar available in a budget that, even by standards of the '30s and '40s, was extremely modest for the job to be done.

The agencies implemented a complete program. It included consumer advertising using newspapers and radio, produce trade advertising, advertising to restaurants, baked potato flags and menu clip-ons, point-of-purchase display material for retail stores, recipe development and food page publicity, direct mail promotion to the grocery trade and dealer service men in the field. As Idaho's market share increased, growers produced more potatoes and the budget grew. Idaho passed up Maine as the largest potato producing state in the nation.

In the meantime Botsford, Constantine & Gardner merged with Ketchum McCloud and Grove and consolidated their west coast business in a San Francisco office as Botsford Ketchum.

The advent of television began to produce mutterings in the Idaho potato industry regarding the IPC advertising program. The grower sector in particular wanted to see Idaho® potatoes advertised on TV. The fact that the budget was inadequate for any kind of a meaningful television campaign made no difference. Almost every home had a TV set and television advertising worked miracles. Attempts to get a bill introduced in the Legislature for an increase in the assessment always met with opposition from one farm organization or another, however.

Representatives from the San Francisco office of Foote Cone & Belding advertising agency, began making calls in Idaho and in February of 1973 an agency review was held with Foote Cone the winner, replacing Botsford Ketchum. The IPC did, however, retain Cline Inc. for local service tasks and in-state public relations.

In contrast to Botsford Ketchum, FC&B did not have a public relations department, so the Idaho Potato Commission went shopping in New York where they awarded their national PR business to Dudley, Anderson, Yutzy, a long-established public relations shop headed by president Barbara Hunter. DAY had considerable experience with food accounts and had good relationships with media that paid off in publicity placements.

Faced with the task of producing television commercials on a small budget, FC&B convinced Idaho governor Cecil D. Andrus to appear in TV commercials as a spokesman for Idaho® potatoes. In spite of the primitive production techniques used for the commercials, the governor's gift of warmth and charisma projected well and when the ads were aired in the nation's large cities they produced a feedback of favorable comments.

The IPC's seven years with Foote Cone & Belding were interrupted by frequent staff changes at the agency office. Norm Anderson was first assigned to the account, only to leave the agency to start his own business. His successor also had a short tenure and FC&B hired Anderson on a consulting basis to handle the Idaho potato account, an arrangement that proved to have its problems. In 1980 the IPC instructed executive director Gordon Randall to have an agency review.

The Commission listened to five major advertising agencies and chose the San Francisco office of D'Arcy, MacManus & Masius to represent them. Tom Allen headed the account team. The advertising campaign began to pick up momentum aided by an increase in the tax to 5¢ per cwt in 1981 which produced a budget of $3,113,325. The extra money afforded more sophisticated TV commercials and double-page, full-color ads in foodservice magazines. And as testimony to the reach of the advertising and PR activities, a survey taken by *The Packer* discovered that the brand,

Idaho® potatoes, was the most recognized nationally.

D'Arcy account executives were also making career moves but, when Sherry Parker was assigned to Idaho® potatoes in 1982, a continuity that was to last nine years was begun. Changes were taking place in Boise too. James W. Davis, who had been active on the account at Cline/Inc. since 1957, moved to W. R. Drake agency and moved the Idaho potato in-state public relations services as well.

In 1985 a merger changed the name to D'Arcy, Masius, Benton & Bowles which became the world's 5th largest advertising agency. That same year the IPC budget had reached $3,600,000 as inflation fueled rising advertising costs.

Mergers and consolidations in client companies and in advertising agencies brought about a great deal of change in four years, and in March of 1989 DMB&B announced that they were closing their San Francisco office. Another agency stood ready to step into the breech, however, and DDB Needham took over the abandoned office and hired several DMB&B employees, among them Sherry Parker who had the responsibility for the Idaho account. The Idaho Potato Commission decided to go along with the new agency.

Don Odiorne was hired by the IPC as vice president for foodservice in 1989 and Sharyl Strongman as foodservice specialist. With the added marketing emphasis on the eating-away-from-home industry, that portion of the advertising account was split off and, after presentations, awarded to Anderson Rothstein in March of 1990. The Anderson was the same Norm Anderson, now with his own

127

business, that had once worked on the Idaho account for FC&B.

In the activities of national public relations and consumer education, Ogilvy and Mather had purchased DAY and reshaped account service policies and personnel. The IPC decided to review national PR firms and Creamer, Dickson & Basford of New York became the new PR practitioners for Idaho® potatoes.

Export business was also being pursued by the Idaho potato industry and the IPC decided to register its trademarks in Japan and attempt to open up that market. To assist in the effort, the Asahi agency was retained to conduct a study for the IPC and assist in the trademark registration process.

With a new PR agency and a new foodservice agency in place, the Commission decided to review the consumer advertising agency service as well. When the review was announced it was to include DDB Needham, but the agency executives made the decision to resign the account and not be a contender in the competitive presentations. The San Francisco office of Young and Rubicam was selected and, at this writing, is conducting its second national advertising campaign for the world's most famous potato.

In general, many talented and dedicated people at the several agencies that have been involved have lent their energies to the advertising and promotion of Idaho® potatoes. With continued success in the market place, the growth of the Idaho potato industry and its promotional programs will only be limited by the quantity of potatoes that can be grown in the Gem State.

With the amount of competition that exists in food marketing, it is extremely unlikely that the Idaho potato industry will ever be without a substantial advertising program and a national advertising agency to plan, create and communicate the Idaho advertising message to the American public.

Chapter X
FIELD MERCHANDISERS
DEVELOP MARKETS
FOR IDAHO® POTATO

By the time Idaho shippers were selling carloads of potatoes in distant cities, the technology of communications made it possible for them to conduct their business by telegraph or telephone.

In many cases, Idaho shippers who sold to produce jobbers in mid-western, southern and eastern cities, contacted them entirely by phone. Buyer and seller never met face-to-face. Since the supply of fresh potatoes available for shipment varied from day-to-day, it was more practical for the seller to be at the shipping point where his knowledge of the availability of the merchandise was firsthand. This replaced the usual selling situation in which a salesman would travel to his customer's place of business and do the selling on a face-to-face basis.

This physical isolation of the seller from his customer pointed to the necessity of having someone making calls in the markets for the Idaho potato industry. When the Idaho Advertising Commission was formed, one of the recommendations made by the advertising agency was to employ a traveling fieldman who would go into major markets and call on brokers, jobbers, carlot receivers and chain store produce merchandisers. The early days of this field merchandising effort, 1937, were undertaken with part-time help. People were hired to represent the Idaho potato industry during the marketing season and names such as Tom L. Watkins, Lloyd Bell and O. A. Kelley appear as early employees of the Idaho commission.

The promotional body finally decided to hire a full-time representative. They selected Cecil G. Rice, who had been working in potato and onion industries in Colorado. "C. G.," as he was known throughout the industry, was probably responsible for setting the pattern that later Idaho field merchandising representatives followed. He bought an automobile, packed his personal belongings and necessities in the trunk and started driving. C. G. maintained no permanent household, but traveled continually around the country and returned to Idaho during the summer season when the industry was not actively marketing fresh potatoes.

The Idaho Potato Commission representatives began participating in United Fresh Fruit and Vegetable Association conventions. This gave Rice and members of the Potato Commission an opportunity to establish the Idaho name with a large number of potential customers in a short period of time. A sizable exhibit area was part of the United Fresh Fruit and Vegetable convention and Idaho early became one of the major exhibitors. C. G. Rice worked with prominent potato grower Joe Marshall and Boise

131

C.G. Rice   Dean Probert   Chuck McDaniel

exhibit designer Jack Eisenberg to produce large displays featuring hundreds of pounds of select Idaho® potatoes.

C. G. Rice had an easy-going, friendly personality and was well received wherever he made calls on Idaho potato customers.

The effects of Rice's sales and public relations efforts became known in Idaho as shippers got reports from their customers that "the Idaho man" had called on them and they were "very pleased with making his acquaintance."

As production increased and larger quantities of potatoes became available to sell, it became obvious that more manpower was needed if an adequate job of covering the country was to be done. To fill this need the Potato Commission hired Dean Probert in July 1953. Dean had been a supermarket manager with the C. C. Anderson chain in Idaho and brought with him retail merchandising experience which was to serve him well in his field job for the Potato Commission.

The Idaho field representatives participated in other

132

conventions which were added to the calendar of annual events. The huge National Restaurant Convention in Chicago became another show place for the Idaho potato exhibit and the Supermarket Institute convention was another regular event. Some years later, the School Lunch Convention was added to the list.

Competition became tougher and field calls more important and in December of 1957 Clyde Domeny was added to the Idaho field staff. Domeny had been schooled in Safeway and Albertson's stores in the Gem State. The field merchandising staff developed a system of making the most important calls in the cities they visited and seeing as many other customers or potential customers as time allowed. They called on produce brokers, jobbers, carlot receivers, produce repackers and chain store buyers and merchandising executives. They often found themselves solving problems for Idaho shippers when a misunderstanding with the customer had developed or a "trouble car" was on the siding in a city that they were visiting.

The Idaho field staff never actually made sales or wrote orders, but their goodwill calls were an important factor in the Idaho promotional program. One of their important jobs was to make the customers aware of the Idaho promotional programs and relay orders for point-of-purchase display material, baked potato flags, recipe folders and other promotional aides that were provided by the Commission. They also made calls on newspapers and radio and television stations in the markets where Idaho potato advertising was run to solicit advertising help from the media. After their scheduled call list of important customers was taken care of in a given city, the Idaho field merchandisers made calls on individual supermarkets and restaurants to gather information and to promote the sale of more Idaho® potatoes.

As a means of communicating with the Idaho potato industry, a weekly market flash was inaugurated. Each of the field merchandisers would phone in a weekly report summarizing the market conditions in the city where he had been making calls. This would provide sales leads to Idaho industry people who were looking for customers. The familiar "market flash" became a very important document to the Idaho shipping industry and later to Idaho processors as it provided a direct information feedback from major markets all over the country.

In June of 1965 C. G. Rice retired from active participation in the field merchandising program because of his health. The routine of constant travel and attendance at conventions proved to be a very demanding one since it involved driving long distances in all kinds of weather conditions as well as making trade calls in the market. Charles "Chuck" McDaniel was hired to replace C. G. Rice that same year and, after a short indoctrination in Idaho, began the gypsy life of living out of his automobile and staying in motels and hotels all over the territory. Domeny, Probert and McDaniel had the company of their wives in their travels. C. G. Rice had always traveled alone.

Idaho produce convention display in the early 1970s.

Milt Maclin   Clyde Domeny   Robert Reichert

As the problem of misrepresentation grew in importance, the field merchandisers on occasion found themselves investigating reports of cheating in the markets. Sometimes repackers would buy used Idaho bags and put cheaper russet potatoes from other production areas in them to be sold at the premium Idaho price. It soon became obvious that the field merchandisers could not act both as policemen and goodwill ambassadors and the work was turned over to specialists.

The selling season for Idaho was roughly from August first to mid-June, giving the field merchandising staff a chance to return to Idaho during mid-summer to discuss problems and opportunities with shippers and members of the Potato Commission and to attend the annual Idaho Grower Shippers Association convention in Sun Valley. The field merchandisers were given an opportunity to address the convention delegates as a regular part of the program for a verbal report of their year's activities and to discuss changes that were taking place in the industry which were of interest to potato shippers.

The death of Dean Probert in 1971 and the resignation of Chuck McDaniel to go into private business created two vacancies in the field merchandising staff. Milt Maclin, who had been employed by the Florida Citrus Commission, and Robert Reichert, former Idaho State Commissioner of Agriculture, were hired by the Commission to continue the field merchandising work. During the first thirty years of the Idaho field merchandising program, the fieldmen were actually employed by the Commission's advertising agency. It was impossible for them to travel to large cities where prices were high and conform to State of Idaho travel expense limitations on food, lodging and mileage. The advertising agencies contracted with the Commission to perform field merchandising services and hired the fieldmen, rebilling their salaries and travel expenses to the Commission.

In 1973 a change in the law, which made the Potato Commission custodian of their own funds, made possible the transfer of the field merchandising activities directly to the Idaho Potato Commission office.

Changing marketing conditions also called for a reassessment of priorities as far as calls were concerned. With produce jobbers and brokers handling a smaller portion of the total volume in the marketing of potatoes, field merchandisers began making calls on chain store buyers and produce merchandising executives and spending less time with the decreasing numbers of produce brokers and jobbers in the major terminal markets. The long-established practice of traveling continually and having no home address was also changed. Milt Maclin took up residence in Dallas, Texas; Robert Reichert named New Jersey as his home base, however keeping his home near Filer, Idaho; and Clyde Domeny established his home in Boise. The change enabled the field staff to live more conventional lives.

The Idaho industry became more and more dependent on the work of the market relations directors (a new title), and requests for additional field activity prompted the Commission to add to the staff. Reichert changed from making market calls and became a PR spokesman for Idaho® potatoes under the direction of Dudley, Anderson, Yutzy, appearing on TV talk shows in major cities. His activities were taken over by George Fisher in the northeast and in 1978 two additional people, William Harper and Frieda Poulos, were hired to work in the midwest and the far western U.S. respectively. Poulos had the distinction of being the first female field representative for Idaho and one of few in the produce industry.

In 1979 Dick Reissig joined the group when George Fisher dropped field work for another produce industry position. In 1980 there were six people in the field; Clyde Domeny, Frieda Poulos, Milt Maclin, Dick Reissig, Bill Harper and the latest addition, Dick Rath.

Clyde Domeny's retirement after two and a half decades of distinguished service and Bill Harper's and Dick Reissig's resignations resulted in the hiring of Bill Hartz in 1984 and the staff became relatively stable until 1989 when Maclin and Rath also retired. The two were replaced by Larry Whiteside in the midwest and Don Luchka in the southeast.

Increasing potato production in Idaho and higher advertising assessment rates provided the IPC with larger budgets which not only made staff additions possible but provided more funds for direct promotional work with retail and foodservice chains.

The market relations directors were aided in the responsibility of foodservice contacts by foodservice director Barbara Bertelli and later by Don Odiorne who replaced Bertelli in 1989 with the title of vice president for foodservice. Sharyl Strongman was added as foodservice specialist and staff dietitian in 1990 later to become foodservice market relations director.

As programs grew, the IPC decided to add a vice president for retail merchandising who would oversee the market relations directors. Jack Hansen left the Washington Apple Commission to fill the Idaho position in February of 1991. Don Luchka resigned that year and William White and William Savilonis, Jr. joined the retail staff to bring the total manpower to six including Hansen.

The Idaho field program has long been regarded as one of the most successful in the nation and has achieved remarkable results, particularly in the early days when it was forced to operate on a tiny budget compared to other commodity programs.

The availability of more money and more people has added greatly to the impact of market representation for

Don Odiorne, vice president, foodservice

Jack Hansen, vice president, retail merchandising

Sharyl Strongman, market relations director, foodservice

the Idaho potato industry and has made possible the targeting of specific markets and specific customers to increase sales of Idaho® potatoes in a more direct way.

Much has changed since C. G. Rice took to the road in his Chevrolet to represent Idaho® potatoes back in the '40s, but the continuity of Idaho's market contact program has never faltered and the contribution that it has made to industry growth and prosperity is a major factor in the success story of the world's most famous potato.

Market relations directors representing the Idaho Potato Commission are: (left to right, top row) Bill Hartz, Larry Whiteside, Bill White. Bottom row, Jim Grimm and William Savilonis, Jr.

Chapter XI
INDUSTRY REVOLUTION
ACCOMPANIES
GROWTH OF
POTATO PROCESSING

The average high school student in Brooklyn, New York, has a limited awareness of the state of Idaho and for good reason. Idaho is a remote western state with only about one-fourth the population of that one New York borough. Idaho is known for potatoes and Sun Valley. It is unusual to find anyone in the eastern United States with more specific knowledge unless they have visited Idaho.

Little does the city dweller realize the extent to which developments in the Idaho potato industry have affected his eating habits. He would never dream that his per capita consumption of potatoes has increased because of developmental work done in this remote and thinly-populated western state.

It is not often that a shot fired in Idaho is heard "around the world," but the potato processing revolution is one that would well qualify.

The earliest form of potato processing, now lost in antiquity, was probably the drying of potatoes to preserve them for later use. In Idaho, the first processing activity was the extraction of starch from potatoes closely followed by the production of potato flour and potato meal.

These activities were primarily adapted for salvaging unusable potatoes or utilizing surplus supplies in low-priced years. Starch plants were never popular with growers because the portion of their crop that went into starch represented a less-than-break-even venture for them.

The Rogers Brothers Seed Company claims the first dehydration of potatoes for food use in Idaho. They indicate that they were producing potato flour in 1926 and drying diced potatoes in 1940.

Military needs during World War II forced the development of techniques that gave birth to the modern potato processing industry in the Gem State as well as the rest of the world.

With supply lines that stretched halfway around the globe, the U.S. Army was vitally interested in reducing the weight and bulk of vegetables used to feed troops. Onion dehydration was already underway in California when the J. R. Simplot Company became interested. Basic Vegetable Corporation had been buying fresh onions in Idaho for drying at their Vacaville plant and Simplot Western Idaho Produce Company was selling supplies to the California processor.

Eager to increase supply capability, the U.S. Quartermaster Corps encouraged the building of an onion dehydration plant and "Jack" Simplot chose a site south of Caldwell adjacent to the onion growing area.

144

Most wartime employees rode the bus to work, few drove cars.

Ray Dunlap, left, developed the frozen french fry for Simplot.

Onions were dried in direct-fired dehydration tunnels using oil as the source of heat. Hot air and products of combustion from the large burners were blown into the tunnels over the exposed surfaces of the minced onions which were spread out on wood slatted dehydration trays. The trays, in turn, were stacked on transfer cars and pushed by hand on rails. As a car of freshly-peeled-and-cut onion pieces entered one end of the tunnel, a car of completely dehydrated onion chips or flakes emerged from the other. The tunnels operated twenty-four hours a day on three shifts, each burner roaring like a small hurricane.

Dehydrated onions were a highly satisfactory product. They reconstituted well and retained the tangy flavor of the Sweet Spanish variety grown in the area. Under forced draft, the burners were clean and a slight sulphur content in the oil provided sulphur dioxide which acted as a preservative.

The army was also eager to lighten the load of potatoes they were shipping to the far corners of the world. They approached Simplot in 1942 and asked him to make some experimental runs on diced Idaho potatoes to determine if the same technique used on onions would yield a satisfactory product.

The tests met government specifications and the process of greatly expanding the Caldwell plant to produce dehydrated potatoes began. Simplot also constructed a dehydrator in Blackfoot and one at Bakersfield, California.

Because dehydrated potatoes were so successful from a

logistical standpoint, American servicemen were over-exposed to the product in army and navy mess halls. Along with powdered eggs and dry milk, dehydrated potatoes came out of World War II with a bad name.

In the meantime, under the auspices of the United States Department of Agriculture, experimentation was proceeding on a powdered, mashed potato product based on an English process. Scientists had discovered that potato cells will separate from each other as complete units when the moisture content of a mixture of mashed, cooked potatoes is sufficiently low. These individual potato cells can then be further dried, preserved for a considerable period of time and reconstituted by the addition of hot or boiling water. This process developed into a product known as instant mashed potatoes or potato granules.

The R. T. French Company, world-wide food distributors with home offices in London, England, introduced instant mashed potatoes to the American consuming public. They first tried a production plant in the eastern United States and later relocated in Shelley, Idaho, where the first Idaho granule plant was built in 1952 to use the English process and English machinery. Encumbered with the bad name that dehydrated potatoes had gained during the war, the new product was slow to catch on.

In the meantime, the war ended and government orders slowed down for dehydrated diced potatoes. The United States involvement in the Korean conflict gave the business an additional life of several more years and then de-

Processors developed the first large potato storage buildings.

Magic Valley Foods first plant in Rupert — 1966.

mand hit an all-time low.

Leon C. Jones had been hired by J. R. Simplot Company as production manager at their Caldwell plant and later became vice president and general manager of the Simplot Company Food Processing Division. He guided the division through the post-war period and began looking for new opportunities in the years ahead to replace existing processed potato products. A crash program of research was undertaken with the idea of developing new potato products which would be acceptable to the housewife and to commercial chefs in American restaurants.

A Simplot food technologist, Ray Dunlap, aimed his efforts at developing products that would make the potato a convenience item in the consumer's kitchen. Various approaches were tried to the problem of supplying French fried potatoes, which were well-liked by American consumers but had the disadvantage of requiring considerable work and time in preparation.

In the meantime, a large ice-making plant had been installed at Caldwell to provide ice for railroad refrigerator cars. This plant provided ice for Pacific Fruit Express cars which were being used for the shipment of perishables to eastern markets. The ice business had a rather short life as mechanical refrigerator cars began to make their appearance and Pacific Fruit Express found their own sources to be adequate. This left the Simplot Caldwell facilities with a freezing capacity of considerable size and no market for the ice that they had been producing.

The convenience and appetite appeal of frozen foods developed a brisk post-war market for many vegetables and fruits and it seemed a natural direction for product research in potatoes. Dunlap first experimented with potatoes cut into French fry strips, water-blanched and frozen. This saved the housewife the peeling and strip cutting operation, but she still needed a deep-fat fryer in her kitchen and a cooking time of about fifteen minutes for comparatively small quantities of French fried potatoes. Faced with an indifferent market reaction to the water-blanched product, Dunlap then tried deep frying the potatoes before freezing. This proved to be the most significant development in the short history of potato processing and gave birth to a product which grew to a volume of billions of dollars each year.

After experimentation with laboratory size quantities of French fried potatoes, the research and development department at the Simplot Caldwell plant decided to make some experiments on production line techniques. For this, they purchased a second-hand fryer that had been employed in a potato chip plant. Grouped around the fryer for the first production run were Vice-President Leon Jones, Food Technologist and Researcher Ray Kueneman, Chemist Ray Dunlap and Production Maintenance Chief and Innovator Spencer Briant. The potatoes were passed through a peeler and through strip cutters and then water-blanched to prepare them for frying. The semi-cooked potato strips were fed over a conveyor into one end of the French fryer and the group waited eagerly at the other end

Potato "rounds" were one of the successful new processed products.

Frozen stuffed, baked potatoes failed to become popular.

to see the emergence of the golden strips of French fried potatoes. They had overlooked one fact, however. Thin-sliced potato chips float to the surface of frying fat, however the French cut strips of potatoes sunk to the bottom of the fryer. As the group waited, not only did no French fries make their appearance at the discharge end of the fryer, but smoke began issuing from the surface of the boiling fat. The French fried potatoes were burning at the bottom of the fryer. More raw strips poured in but no finished French fries appeared as the burned strips accumulated.

Despite this temporary disappointment, the research and development team continued their efforts to produce French fried potatoes on a production line basis. The black iron fryer proved to have another disastrous limitation. Cast iron in contact with hot frying fat produced a chemical reaction which caused the frying medium to break down rapidly and rancidity to develop. A fryer load of vegetable shortening had a very short life and the odor which emitted from the fryer as the fat began to break down was almost impossible for employees to tolerate in the production line area.

Quantities of the potato product that did find a way satisfactorily through the frying process and were quick frozen received a somewhat more enthusiastic market acceptance than previous products. This encouraged the Simplot research team to commission the design of a fryer specifically engineered for the production of French fried potatoes. The problem of the sinking potato strips was solved by the invention of an oscillating basket system which lifted and advanced the potato strips through the boiling shortening until they reached the discharge end of the fryer and were picked up by a conveyor screen. The solution to the breakdown problem was to use stainless steel for the construction of the fryer and all of its parts. This noncorrosive metal did not produce the chemical reaction which broke down the frying fat. A centrifuge system was added to clean the liquid shortening on a continuing basis.

This development established a reasonable economic basis for frozen French fried potatoes since entire fryer loads of shortening did not have to be discarded. The constant cleaning of the frying medium kept it in fresh condition. Shortening was added only as the potato strips absorbed it and the problems that had plagued the process earlier were essentially solved.

At the same time, other food processors in the Idaho area had heard of the Simplot work and were becoming interested in the processing of potatoes as well. As the development of the frozen French fried potato was going forth in Caldwell, Ore-Ida Foods in Ontario, Oregon, were experimenting with another potato product — a frozen, shredded potato patty. Ore-Ida built their first plant in 1951. Both the frozen French fries and frozen potato patties were successful as retail items. National private brand distributors of frozen foods became interested and had the two companies produce the new products for them to sell under their own labels.

The major problem confronting Idaho's potato processors in the distribution of new products was lack of available space in supermarket frozen food counters. Already filled with a number of frozen fruits and vegetables, frozen juice concentrates and a number of other new items, it became difficult to get retailers interested in a relatively low-priced frozen potato product.

Processors began investigating the possibility of frozen French fried potatoes for use in restaurants. Visits to restaurant kitchens in various cities established the fact that most potatoes were being handled badly by restaurant personnel and that the American public was seldom served a really good French fried potato in a commercial restaurant. Refinement in the processing of frozen French fries made some very significant improvements in flavor, texture, color and digestibility of this international favorite. This gave the frozen French fries processed in Idaho a distinct quality advantage over the food that the average restaurant chef could put on the plate starting with raw potatoes. It also significantly reduced preparation time and labor expense in the institutional kitchen.

Simplot's answer to the needs of the restaurant industry was a special institutional package which contained thirty pounds of frozen French fry strips. Although the French fries in consumer packages were fried to a nearly-finished color because they were designed to be heated in the oven by the housewife, the restaurant kitchen was equipped with a fryer and could reconstitute the frozen French fried potatoes much more

154

quickly and with a better flavor and texture.

The first lots of institutional French fries were prepared to the finished color that the retail product had demanded. This proved to be a problem since the restaurant cook could simply not adapt to the idea of removing a
basket of French fries from the deep-fat fryer after they
had been in the boiling fat for as short a time as a min-
ute-and-a-half. The product began to find acceptance
when the institutional color was held back to a partially-
cooked state and the restaurant cook was required to fry
the potatoes slightly longer to develop the golden skin
which appeals to the consumer's eye. Although acceptance and growth of demand seemed slow in the initial
stages, frozen French fried potatoes has been one of the
outstanding food product successes of all time.

The improved quality and convenience of this item soon
made it the number-one selling item in frozen food departments of most supermarkets. Restaurants and institutions across the country also converted to the use of
frozen French fried potatoes very rapidly.

New processors entered the field and existing ones built
new plants and expanded production facilities each year
in an attempt to keep up with the burgeoning demand.
Along with a growth and demand for frozen French fried
potatoes, a number of other frozen specialty products were
developed.

Ore-Ida Foods introduced an extruded-shredded item
that they named Tater Tots and other processors soon
developed their own versions. It was deep fried and had

155

the flavor and eye appeal needed to make it an almost instant success.

Although the original concept of frozen French fries was for one size and style of cut, this first model was soon joined by a crinkle-cut strip which was appealing to the eye and exposed more potato surface to the frying fat to provide additional fried potato flavor. Cuts and sizes proliferated until the institutional customer could find almost any style and size to suit a personal whim.

While demand for frozen potato products was growing at a rapid rate, research and processing improvements had made the dehydrated potato granule into a highly-acceptable mashed potato. Not only was the United States government buying large quantities for military use, but the R. T. French Company was experiencing some success with retail packages of instant potatoes and the restaurants and institutions were switching to instant mashed as a convenient way of serving this American favorite.

Meanwhile, a new product had been developed by the United States Department of Agriculture — dehydrated potato flakes. Flakes provided another means of preparing mashed potatoes. The dehydrated flakes were reconstituted in much the same way as potato granules and although the flakes did not have the density of potato granules, this relatively greater bulk proved to be an advantage for consumer packages. A larger-looking package of dehydrated potatoes could be sold in flake form and the housewife found it difficult to believe that she was get-

This plant in Burley, Idaho , was built in one of the early attempts to produce instant mashed potatoes. The tower, which was intended to be used in the drying process, failed to work as planned. The plant was later purchased by J.R.Simplot Co. and a fluidized bed process installed. Now shut down, the building is used as a warehouse.

ting the same amount of finished product from potato granules. Flakes also proved to be easier to prepare because they did not require as careful measurement of water and dehydrated potatoes to produce satisfactory end results.

Since the development work and the early marketing had primarily been done by Idaho processors, Idaho had a distinct time advanatage over other potato producing areas. The building of processing facilities in other growing areas, however, soon created a situation of competition. The inherent excellence of the Russet Burbank variety carries through into the processed form, and this virtually forced other potato producing areas to grow russets for processing rather than attempt to process their traditional varieties.

The demand for frozen French fries grew at such a rapid rate that Idaho processors found they needed to construct additional plants to supply their customers. Rather than tie their entire supply base to one growing area, processors looked afield, and some of the additional capacity was developed in other states, a pattern that includes most of the large processing companies now operating in Idaho.

The impact of potato processing on the Idaho industry stimulated rapid expansion in the growing sector. Desert land was reclaimed in huge projects and growers found processor contracts available which provided a hedge and guaranteed them a market for their crops.

Since the processors wanted to operate their plants twelve months a year, if possible, the need to store mountainous quantities of raw potatoes became obvious.

The University of Idaho College of Agriculture had done extensive research on storing potatoes at the Aberdeen station under the direction of Professor Walter Sparks. The technology was in great demand and proved to be expandable to the football-field sized storage buildings that growers and processors built on many farms and plant sites throughout the growing area.

Growers also found it necessary to follow the latest in scientific cultural practices to meet the specifications of the processing industry. Agronomists from processor raw product departments worked with growers on an almost daily basis to insure the quantity and quality of the harvest.

The popularity of frozen potato products grew quickly and recently when it appeared that the peak had been reached, processors introduced a variety of new items. Typical of them are pre-formed frozen hash browns, curly fries, frozen mashed potatoes and seasoned fries.

There were also a number of purely dehydration plants built. They dried spuds to produce instant mashed potato granules, flakes, and variations of dehydrated diced potatoes for soups, stews, au gratin, hash browns and similar products. These plants were located primarily in areas that grew and packed for the fresh potato market because the smaller tubers and those with knobs or irregular shapes, that could not be included in fresh pack containers, made highly acceptable raw product for the dehydrators who bought this processor grade from fresh shippers.

In the late 1970s and early 1980s the dehydration industry saw a large, new market develop for dehydrated

159

potato flakes to be used in the production of snack foods. Procter and Gamble introduced Pringles, a formed potato chip made from potato flakes. Suddenly flakes were in demand for a variety of flavored chips and similar snacks that the American public readily adopted. The flake production capacity in Idaho was multiplied in a short span of time.

A portion of the credit for new product development belongs to Miles Willard, an Idaho Falls chemical engineer and food processing specialist, who has developed new items made from Idaho® potatoes for some of the largest potato processors and snack food manufacturers. Two of Willard's most visible successes are Keebler's O'Boisies potato chips and Ore-Ida's Toaster Fries™.

PROCESSING COMPANIES OPERATING IN IDAHO AT THIS WRITING INCLUDE:
Basic American Foods
> Producers of dehydrated products with plants located at Blackfoot, Rexburg and Idaho Falls

Nestle' Brands
> Producers of frozen and dehydrated products with a plant located at Nampa

Idaho Fresh-Pak, Inc
> Producers of dehydrated products with plants located at Lewisville and Idaho Falls

Idaho Pacific Corporation
> Producers of dehydrated products with a plant located at Ririe

Idaho Supreme Potatoes, Inc.
Producers of dehydrated products with a plant located at Firth

Lamb-Weston
Producers of frozen products with a plant located at American Falls

Larsen of Idaho
Producers of dehydrated products with a plant located at Hamer

Magic West, Inc.
Producers of frozen and dehydrated products with a plant located at Glenns Ferry

Magic Valley Foods, Inc.
Producers of frozen and dehydrated products with a plant located at Rupert

Nonpareil Corporation
Producers of dehydrated products with a plant located at Blackfoot

Ore-Ida Foods, Inc.
Producers of frozen products with a plant located at Burley

The Pillsbury Co.
Producers of dehydrated products with a plant located at Shelley

J. R. Simplot Company
Producers of frozen and dehydrofrozen products with plants located at Caldwell, Heyburn and Aberdeen

Sun-Glo of Idaho, Inc.

Producers of frozen products with a plant located at Rexburg

Universal Frozen Foods

Producers of frozen products with a plant located at Twin Falls

Western Idaho Potato Processing Co.

Producers of frozen products with a plant located at Nampa

Chapter XII
CAREY LAND ACT TRANSFORMS DESERT INTO POTATO FIELDS

The first significant irrigation project in the West developed as a grim struggle for survival and interestingly enough the water was diverted to irrigate potatoes. In 1847 the first band of Mormon pioneers, having traveled many miles to a remote valley, built a small dam across City Creek near the present site of the Mormon Temple in Salt Lake City. They succeeded in diverting sufficient water to saturate some five acres of land. Before the day was over they had planted their potatoes in an effort to preserve the seed.

This single event was the beginning of western irrigation as it is practiced today.

The Mormon people by nature and by church rule operated as a cooperative community. The Mormon system of issuing shares for water and attaching water rights to the land are basic to irrigation control today. The development of irrigation in Utah by the Mormons remained for some years the only substantial private irrigation enterprise in the western states. Until 1870 no large amounts of land were under irrigation except 154,000 acres reported cultivated by Mormon settlers in 1865.

In Idaho the Mormon communities were not so concentrated and the efforts of individual farmers to put water on their land were too costly. Adding to the problems was a lack of technical know-how. Land easy to irrigate next to natural waterways was quickly settled, but the many arid acres beyond proved a unique challenge for the Idaho farmer.

Perhaps the most important action taken nationally in behalf of irrigation in Idaho was the Carey Act of August, 1894. Under the Carey Act, the so-called public land states with desert lands were offered one million federal acres each, provided they would cause the granted lands to be irrigated.

Idaho benefited from the Carey Act far more than did any other state — about 60% of all the lands irrigated in the United States under the Carey Act are in Idaho.

The construction of the Carey Act was actually three fold and included three contracts: first, involving the federal government and the state; second, the state and the construction company; and finally, the construction company and the settlers on the project. It was a unique scheme never before attempted in the United States whereby private enterprise would construct the irrigation works under state supervision and initially finance projects by mortgaging its equity in the project, issuing bonds or assigning its contracts with the settlers for the purchase of water rights. The ultimate profit would be

164

Early Utah and Idaho settlers lived simply, worked hard.

Hauling the biggest load of potatoes to town was a feat.

derived from the sale of perpetual water rights to settlers on the project.

One of the most important characteristics of the Act was that it required reclamation by irrigation, occupation and cultivation before a patent would be issued--unless as provided by the 1896 amendment, sufficient water was available in substantial ditches or reservoirs to reclaim the lands.

One of the fullest descriptions of the developments and consequences of the Carey Act in Idaho was written as a special report by Mikel H. Williams, a research assistant with the Idaho Department of Reclamation, in 1970. His very extensive and complete study of the effects of the Carey Act nationally and his thorough investigation of each project in Idaho provides a great deal of information and insight into the history of irrigation in Idaho.

Over a period of forty years, sixty-four Carey proposals were filed with the State Land Board of Idaho. The determination of the success or failure of the Carey Act in Idaho is difficult to generalize about for there are many factors to be considered. Of great importance was the fact that the state of Idaho received 618,000 acres of previously desert, arid land. But the overall benefit from the construction of dams and canals, the settlement of farms, the birth of towns and cities and the production of crops on the economy of Idaho is impossible to measure.

The problems Idaho had with the Carey Act stem from two sources, according to Williams: the cost of financing a

166

project and after a project was completed, of supplying the land with adequate water for reclamation. A review of Idaho's sixty-four projects illustrates that almost every project exceeded the estimated cost of construction. In fact, the general rule was that the final cost was double the original estimate.

After a substantial number of failures of construction companies, it became increasingly difficult to finance a Carey project or to complete those already under construction. In the early 1900s the problem became so acute that it was almost impossible to sell bonds to the general public or to find people willing to invest as stockholders in a construction company. As more companies failed, less investors could be found, and being unable to secure additional funds to complete the projects already underway, more companies went bankrupt or had their contracts with the State of Idaho forfeited. This caused the general public to become even more wary of investing its money in any type of Carey Act undertaking.

The other factor in the failure of the Carey Act was the almost total lack of information as to the available water supply for a particular undertaking. The irrigation engineer was unknown and comprehensive knowledge of stream flow and annual runoff was almost nonexistent.

According to Mikel Williams, the main problems encountered in the operation and administration of the Carey Act, lack of funds and water, were not inherent defects in the Carey Act itself, but rather the result of poor planning and lack of adequate information.

167

Early potato land had to be flat enough for gravity irrigation.

Hand potato picking after tractors replaced horses for digging.

The most successful and famous Carey Act project was the Twin Falls South Side Project located in Twin Falls and Cassia Counties. The estimated cost of the project was $1,500,000, but the final cost amounted to $3,600,000.

The original proposal was filed in October of 1900 by a group of wealthy financiers from Pittsburgh, Pennsylvania, who had plans for reclaiming some 250,000 acres of land. By 1932 the project was operating efficiently except for some seepage problems and some reconstruction on the Milner Dam. At that time 192,750 acres had been reclaimed. From the standpoint of the settlers, the construction company and the state, the project was termed a success. The most important contribution of the Twin Falls South Side Project was that it proved that reclamation was feasible on a wide scale. Only one mortgage was given by the construction company and it was soon paid off. The success of this project spurred new Carey Act developments in the state and with them came money and people.

The success of the South Side Project was a definite incentive for developers of new projects. Two of the most ambitious promoters were the Kuhn brothers from Pittsburgh. In approximately fifteen months the Kuhns started three Carey Act projects and segregated 199,552 acres of desert land. Each of their projects adopted the name "Twin Falls" in an effort to trade on the reputation of their earlier success.

None of the Kuhn-sponsored projects developed as well as the original Twin Falls project did. Of the three, the

Twin Falls North Side Project had the greatest success with patent acres at 178,062.17 after many problems and only a reduction of 85,000 acres from the segregated acreage.

All three projects were completed but each suffered a tremendous reduction of patent acreage because of limited water availability. The total of acres segregated for the three projects numbered more than 400,000, yet the patented acres totaled just over 200,000.

Carey Act reclamation projects have put substantial tracts of land under cultivation that became family farms and were utilized to grow Idaho® potatoes. Without this one piece of legislation many of today's potato fields would be range for cattle and sheep.

Once water is available, houses, power lines and roads follow.

Chapter XIII
HIGH-LIFT PUMPING CREATES
SNAKE RIVER LAND RUSH

One of the most significant developments in the Idaho potato industry in recent years has been the greatly increased acreage of farm land planted to potatoes. Although tracts of land have been reclaimed and added to Idaho's irrigated acreage in all parts of the Snake River watershed, by far the largest additions have come on the south side of the river down stream from Twin Falls. Most of this newly cultivated land has been brought into production by groups of individuals who have filed under the Desert Land Entry Act.

Formerly federal land held by the Bureau of Land Management, these thousands of acres of desert became eligible to be claimed when water for irrigation could be shown to be available. When the feasibility of irrigating these desert tracts was demonstrated, desert entry claims were filed by the hundreds, creating a land rush which rivaled those of an earlier day in American history.

As is so often the case, the entire progression of events was triggered by a great idea whose time had come. The

172

vision and the imagination of one man resulted in the development of half a dozen or more individual projects, the largest of which reclaimed more than 25,000 acres in one development.

It is true that desert entry filings accounted for the greatest portion of the reclamation activity but, curiously enough, the initial project land did not come from that source. Shortly following World War I the Boise-Kuna Land Development Project was completed under the Bureau of Reclamation. Included in that project was a tract south of Nampa known as the Dry Lake area. The name comes from an extremely flat basin with a surface composed of bentonite. During the wet season of the year, a few inches of water collects over the virtually impenetrable bentonite and creates a small temporary lake. Freezing to the bottom in the wintertime, the sheet of ice was a popular skating spot for Boise Valley youth in December and January of the most severe winters. In the spring, after the rainy season, the water quickly evaporated and it became, in fact, a dry lake.

After the development of the Boise-Kuna irrigation project, it was found that there were more acres involved than there was water available to irrigate. Because of its location and elevation, the Dry Lake area was not included in the early development and failed to get the irrigation water that had been promised.

In the meantime, eager homesteaders had filed their claims and established their homesteads awaiting the coming of the irrigation canals to begin farming. Having

Allen Noble with sprinklers at Dry Lake project.

fulfilled the homestead requirements, patents were granted on the farms although they were never put into production. Many of the homesteaders were not able to keep up the taxes and the lands reverted to the county to be sold for taxes. Others maintained their ownership in the hopes that someday the fertility of the soil would be unlocked by the availability of water and their 30-year dream would become a reality.

As it turned out, water came to the Dry Lake region not through the activities of the Bureau of Reclamation, but through the ingenuity of a young Nampa businessman, Allen Noble, who had been raised on a farm and gone into the farm implement business in Nampa, Idaho. Noble met many farmers and land owners in the area through his business.

One day he was quite unexpectedly offered a parcel of land in the Dry Lake area for $25 an acre. Noble knew that no water was available for the land but, since the individual seemed quite anxious to dispose of it, he condescended to visit the area and look at the sagebrush covered tract.

Another Nampa area farmer, Elmer Tiegs, had purchased an acreage in the Dry Lake area and had drilled wells to supply water. The underground water proved to be a solution to the problem with marginal economics. The wells had to be drilled to nearly 700 feet in depth and the water supply proved to be limited. The long water lift and the limited supply made the advisability of further Dry Lake development from wells highly questionable.

175

While inspecting the area, Noble was impressed by the fertility of the land that Tiegs had brought under cultivation, but discouraged by the lack of availability of underground water. While on the site, he drove his pickup across the tract to the point where the plateau ended at rimrock 500 feet above the Snake River. Noble looked off the edge of the cliff at the green waters flowing in the Snake and asked the question, "Who owns the rights to all of that water flowing down the Snake River?" The Idaho Power Company was currently in the process of constructing three dams downstream in Hells Canyon for the generation of electrical power and the answer was given that the water rights probably belonged to the Idaho Power Company.

Noble returned to his farm implement business and found himself thinking about the Dry Lake situation for the next several days. The Snake River was only 500 feet below the plateau and water was being raised distances equal to that in the Columbia Basin project where he had inspected pumping stations and penstock installations. Upon investigation, he found that the Idaho Power Company did indeed have rights to Snake River water for the generation of electrical power, but water for domestic use and for irrigation use assumed an automatic first and second priority over that of generating power. He began talking to irrigation engineers and equipment manufacturers about the feasibility of an installation at the river to pump water up to the thirsty acres on the Dry Lake plateau.

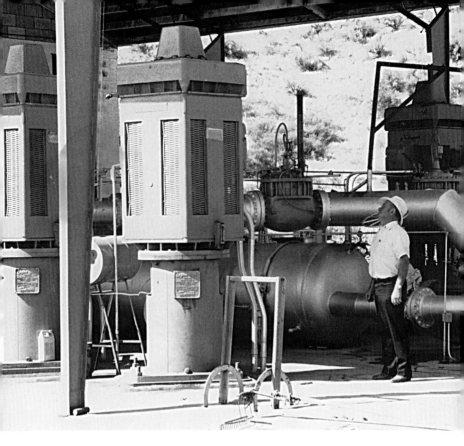

This pumping station on the Snake River supplies irrigation water for the Grindstone Butte and Sailor Creek projects which include a total of 17,524 acres. The pumps are powered by electricity which has increased dramatically in cost since the projects were put in. Economics and water availability make similar high-lift developments in the future unlikely.

Preliminary calculations indicated to Noble that the project was too big for him to handle alone, so he induced a couple of farmer friends, Bob Morris and Dale Jones, to buy some land next to the parcel which he had subsequently purchased and join him in the project. One of the major reasons that the Dry Lake development had waited so many years was the lack of electric motors, pumps and water lifting technology that could meet the engineering requirements of the situation. The availability of sufficient electrical energy at feasible irrigation pumping rates was another factor that had only become a reality in recent years.

Although Noble found that the price of the land he purchased had risen from $25 to $125 when the news got out that the project was going to be a reality, he did make the purchase and by winter of 1961-62 had 640 acres of level sandy-loam soil ready for farming.

Another personality that figured strongly in the Dry Lake development was an experienced pipeline construction contractor, Jack Collins, who had come to the Boise Valley area a few years earlier with the construction of a natural gas pipeline. Many people looked at the precarious rocky canyon wall that rose above the Snake River and said that the construction of a penstock would be "impossible," "prohibitively expensive" or "foolhardy." After consulting several construction firms, Noble had Collins inspect the project and was assured without hesitation that it would be a comparatively simple one. In addition to his knowledge and experience, Collins' es-

178

timate of construction costs was about half of other bids obtained on the job which enabled the three partners to obtain financing and begin construction. The whine of the Dry Lake project pumps was no sooner a reality when another project adjacent to the original one was put into operation by the Basin Land Company. This was another group of developers anxious to get into agriculture on new acres.

As had been the case in other areas of the Snake River Valley, potatoes were the primary crop planted on the new land. With sufficient fertilizer, the desert soil which was rich in trace minerals produced beautiful crops of Idaho russets in the early years following reclamation. The unusually high return from a good crop of potatoes allowed a quick repayment of borrowed money on reclamation projects making them an attractive investment. With increasing populations and the progressive marketing of the Idaho potato industry, potato demand was increasing each year. Although some potato producing areas in the United States were suffering, the market seemed to absorb the increased production of the famous Idaho russet without major problems.

Experience on the Dry Lake project indicated that the costs would be something in excess of $200 per acre. Early potato crops yielded 400 bags per acre with ease, so it did not take many years to pay off the huge investment required in projects of this kind. The new developers found help in their financing from a California-based irrigation company that wanted to develop a market for sprinkler

Smaller pumps create pressure for sprinklers.

pipe and from the Idaho First National Bank, long considered a promoter of agricultural expansion in the Gem State.

The Dry Lake development became an instant topic of conversation throughout the Idaho potato industry. Many growers were aware of the fact that uncounted thousands of acres of fertile desert land lay on the plateaus to the south of the Snake River. With the engineering feasibility of high lift projects established, development possibilities of new farm land seemed without limit. Enthusiastic support was received from the Idaho Power Company whose newly created generating capacity in the Hells Canyon area found a market in the astronomical amounts of electrical energy that 1,500 horsepower pumps consumed during the growing season. The irrigation load was a natural for the Idaho Power Company since they were able to market their capacity in the winter months through the northwest power pool when heating, lighting and other domestic uses peaked demand.

No sooner was Dry Lake in production than Noble and his associates began looking further up the river for additional development possibilities. They found a large tract of desert land in the Sailor Creek area which had been used as a bombing and gunnery range during World War II but was no longer used by the United States Air Force and was available for desert entry filing. Forming a group of friends and associates which included farmer-irrigation engineer J. T. Newcomb, the Sailor Creek project progressed quickly from concept through a feasibility study and a block of claims were filed with the Bureau of Land Management. Sailor Creek presented an even more difficult engineering feat in that the water had to be lifted 725 feet from the Snake River.

The electric motors that powered the pumps were among the largest that had been put into use in Idaho. They were 1,250 horsepower each. The pumps were manufactured by the Worthington Pump Company and were capable of developing the 450 pounds of pressure necessary to force the water up to the 725 foot elevation. The penstock was thirty-six inch steel pipe through which 30,700 gallons of water per minute could be pumped to the distribution system on the plateau. The new concept of the Sailor Creek project was the substitution of pressuriz-ed pipe lines to distribute the water to the fields instead of open ditches. Completely underground, the system of welded and coupled pipes consisted of nearly sixty-five miles of main and lateral lines ranging from thirty-six inch penstock to three inch laterals. Sailor Creek initially brought in 3,750 acres of new land and again a high-lift project became the enthusiastic topic of conversation among Idaho potato growers and land developers all over the state.

When Sailor Creek became a reality, feverish activity in the development of additional desert entry projects con-stituted a veritable land rush. Sailor Creek was quickly followed by the Billy Rio Ranch, the Cottonwood Canal project, the Indian Hills project and Black Mesa.

Indian Hills had one interesting innovation in that the

182

Natural gas powered irrigation pumps.

After centuries of sagebrush, potatoes are grown under sprinklers.

developers chose to use natural gas as an energy source for pumping water rather than electricity. Natural gas was burned in huge internal combustion engines which powered the pumps and the gas distribution company became a competitor of the Idaho Power Company in the marketing of an excess summer pipeline capacity of natural gas.

The Indian Hills project seemed to carry an omen of ill fortune from the beginning which virtually ended the desert entry reclamation activities by causing the Bureau of Land Management to put a freeze on granting desert entry claims.

When the pipeline and pumping station at Indian Hills was completed, the engines were started for the first test. The water was pumped into the pipeline and up to the mesa above. At that point the project engineers were satisfied that the system would work and shut off the gas engines. For some unknown reason, the system designers had not put check valves in the pipelines and as the water in the penstock ran back down to the level of the Snake River, the great weight of the rushing water turned the impellers in the pumps backward, also running the natural gas engines backward and creating extensive damage. Indian Hills also proved to have water distribution problems: canals had been designed without sufficient checks and water proved to be difficult to control with flooding in some areas to a depth of three and four feet.

As a result of the initial problems that developed, Indian Hills entrymen were not able to hold their project together financially and an additional investment was necessary for redesign and rebuilding of the project. At this point the Hood Construction Company entered the picture and supplied technical assistance and money to rescue Indian Hills. It was this corporate intervention which disenchanted the Bureau of Land Management under the premise that Indian Hills was no longer a project owned by individual entrymen exercising their birthright, but by a corporation that had gained title to a large area of low-priced government land. A controversy developed that stalled further desert entry projects for some years.

The Indian Hills situation was finally resolved by the BLM requiring the Hood Construction Company to remove their pumps and property from the project and the land reverted to desert pasture yet to fulfill the green promise of irrigated potato fields.

The largest of the Snake River Plateau projects, and one that showed great promise initially, was the Bell Rapids project. Taking its name from the area on the Snake River where the primary pumping plant was located, Bell Rapids was to bring water to 25,000 acres south of the Snake River opposite the town of Hagerman. The extent of the project was such that it occupied most of the area across the river between the communities of Hagerman and Bliss. As the Snake River land rush got underway, ambitious entrymen began exploring the desert areas very thoroughly.

The originators of the Bell Rapids project were reported

to have ridden over the greater part of the plateau south of the Snake River on motorcycles. This area had the preliminary appearance of good land because of the luxuriant growth of brush and comparatively flat topography. Thorough exploration, soil sampling and formal surveys followed and an engineering feasibility study recommended the development of this largest reclamation project to be privately financed. The water lifts at Bell Rapids vary in the three pumping plants which serve the project. The highest lift is 625 feet. Bell Rapids involves a pumping energy requirement of 50,835 horsepower. Thirteen miles of canals were constructed and 120 miles of buried steel pipe installed.

Another indication of the ambitious planning and scope of Bell Rapids is the fact that 9,000 acres were put under solid-set irrigation systems. Although requiring larger initial investment, solid-set irrigation eliminates sprinkler moving during the growing season and makes control of soil moisture and soil temperature easier.

The development of sprinkler projects the size of Bell Rapids is obviously not limited to growing potatoes. Crop rotation makes the production of alternate crops such as wheat, barley, alfalfa and sugar beets a necessity.

The elevation and climatic conditions of the plateau south of the Snake River are favorable for the growing of most Idaho farm commodities. The growing season is of sufficient length for the potato farmer to achieve 400-sack yields as a routine expectation. The average potato yield for the state of Idaho is somewhere between 200 and 300

The Bell Rapids development spreads across the plateau.

The first pumping plant can be seen at river level.

hundredweight per acre.

The economic impact of a project such as Bell Rapids on the surrounding area is one of increased population, increased employment, increased payment of taxes and a stimulus to all related services and commercial activity. Bell Rapids statistics are impressive in that the property tax paid on the 25,000 acres averages $100,000. During the peak of the growing season, as many as 2,500 people are employed in direct and supporting services. The value of the agricultural crops produced will vary greatly with market prices although, at the time the project was completed, Idaho Power Company estimated the annual production value at $20,000,000.

Bell Rapids had another interesting attribute in that many of the entrymen involved were not professional farmers as such. Under the Desert Entry Act, any U. S. citizen is entitled to file on desert land and the Idaho projects have tended to involve friends, business associates, family members and relatives. It is quite possible for a professional or businessman to become a desert entryman, fulfill all the requirements of the law and hire a farm management specialist to supervise the production of agricultural crops on the desert entry land.

Allen Noble, one of the three original high-lift reclamation developers, is president of a Boise-based company called Farm Development Corporation. A considerable acreage of the Bell Rapids project was initially managed by Farm Development through contractual arrangements. Interestingly enough, Jack

189

Collins, the pipeline contractor who had built many of the Idaho high-lift projects and a good many of those in the Columbia Basin in Washington, was an entryman in the Bell Rapids project where he and his wife filed on the permitted acreage of desert land. G. T. Newcomb, project manager for the development of Bell Rapids, was listed as one of the persons claiming a homestead. Project attorney K. G. Bergquist was also an entryman. Although Bell Rapids showed early promise of becoming the model of high-lift projects, problems developed that affected the profitability for the owners.

The irrigation system proved to have design flaws, and pest and disease problems along with a shortage of water have made it necessary for much of the acreage to be utilized for crops other than potatoes. More storage facilities were built than present production can utilize and some are now unused.

A later addition to desert entry projects in Idaho was one contiguous to the Sailor Creek project called Grindstone Butte. Grindstone Butte had the advantage of the experience acquired during the development of Sailor Creek and the land was of equal quality with the same potential for agricultural productivity. Potato production is still a major factor at Grindstone and Sailor Creek, and the per-acre yields rank with the highest in the state. There has also been considerable crop diversification with mint being a recent addition to the rotation cycle.

Several factors entered the high-lift pumping project picture, however, that discouraged further development.

With the advent of rising prices the later projects rose correspondingly in development cost. Pumping equipment, water distribution systems, access roads, laterals and sprinkler systems all became more expensive until development costs reached more than $300 per acre on the later projects. Continued high prices for agricultural products might have made future projects possible until the oil embargo and the disastrous increases in energy costs in 1974 made new investments in high-lift pumping impractical.

The cost of electrical energy for pumping increased sevenfold from the rates that were in effect when the projects were put in. The evolution of project ownership also proved to be a function of economics. The entrymen who were not well financed found that they could not survive several years of low farm prices and most sold out to neighbors. The projects now typically are owned by two or three farmers who run large, efficient operations.

At the time the projects went in, there was a surplus of water in the Snake River and it seemed that Idaho farmers could continue to reclaim huge tracts of desert. That situation has changed, however, as all the water has been claimed for agriculture, power generation, city water supplies, and the maintenance of migratory fish runs. If a new development were to be proposed, there would be no water on which the project owners could file for the irrigation of crops.

Since corporations were not allowed under the law to file on desert entry land, when two of the state's largest food

Mark Noble, Farm Development Corporation manager at Grindstone Butte and Sailor Creek, checks a hill of Shepody potatoes grown for a processor under contract. Potatoes are now grown in a long rotation cycle but still produce high yields after 20 years of farming the desert entry land.

processors decided to develop high-lift pumping projects, it was necessary for them to find tracts of deeded land that could be purchased and put under irrigation. The J. R. Simplot Company acquired an area above the Payette River where they reclaimed 2,500 acres of desert land with a 440-foot water lift. Ore-Ida Foods, a division of the H. J. Heinz Company, crossed the state line into Oregon and developed Skyline Farms in Malheur County. Both projects were similar in concept to the Snake River projects, but neither seemed blessed with the fertile soil that the entrymen found at Sailor Creek and Bell Rapids.

As a result, both Payette Farms and Skyline Farms met with indifferent success for their corporate developers as far as agricultural productivity was concerned. The Simplot company converted the Payette Farm company to orchards for the growing of apples and purchased Skyline Farms from the H. J. Heinz Company, only to sell it again to finally become the site for a new Oregon state prison.

The fifteen-year period of high-lift irrigation development in Idaho saw an era of history develop in a unique and interesting way. Governmen-sponsored and financed reclamation projects were responsible for most of the large acreage land reclamation in the early days. After the development of the Bureau of Reclamation projects, the next growth increment came primarily from areas of desert which were irrigated from deep wells with pumping from the huge aquifer that underlies the Snake River drainage. The nature of the land and the cost of well drilling limited this type of reclamation to individual projects which never reached the spectacular size of the ones developed by pumping water from the Snake River itself. With private financing replacing large expenditures of federal money, these most recent reclamation projects were brought into production without involving the United States taxpayer.

Two financial institutions contributed greatly to land development along the Snake River. They were the Idaho First National Bank (now West One) and the Northwest Mutual Insurance Company. Typical financial arrangements involved Northwest Mutual lending entrymen the long-term money for the development of the project, and Idaho First National making the short-term loans to individual entrymen for the development of their tracts.

The combination of private citizens and private lending institutions expanding the agricultural economy of Idaho by adding significantly to potato production must certainly be included in the history of the industry. It is one of the noteworthy eras in the story of the potato in Idaho, an era, however, that belonged to the past when there was plentiful desert entry land, cheap energy and lower development costs.

194

Chapter XIV
INDUSTRY CHANGES WITH TECHNOLOGICAL DEVELOPMENTS

When white men first came to Idaho to farm, the heavy work of soil preparation, planting, cultivation and harvesting was done by the muscle power of men and horses. Women also helped out in the fields, but there was usually plenty of hard work to do around the farm house as well.

The internal combustion engine produced the first technological revolution in the Idaho potato industry. Gasoline-powered farm tractors and motor trucks made their appearance about the same time in the early 1920s. Horses continued to play an important role for some time and teams were used for hauling after they had been replaced by the tractor for the heavy work of plowing, cultivating and digging potatoes. In 1920 there were 41,000 acres of potatoes harvested in Idaho at an average yield of 108 hundredweight per acre.

The early potato fields were small by present day standards. Many farmers grew less than ten acres and anyone who had a twenty-acre potato field was considered a big grower. At first, the same farm implements that had been used with horses were simply attached to the draw bar on the new steel-wheeled tractors and pulled through the field in the same way. Frequently this arrangement required one person to drive the tractor and one to sit on the plow, cultivator or whatever the machine happened to be. Growers soon found that they could handle larger acreages of potatoes with the tireless iron tractor. It would work from dawn to dusk and patiently remain out in the field all night waiting for the next day's work to begin.

Idaho's farm-to-market roads were primitive in those early days and in rainy or snowy weather they could become virtually impassable to automobiles and trucks. Growers from Idaho Falls frequently hauled potatoes to town in bobsleds during the snowy winter months with two or more teams providing the power. Early potato planting and harvesting machines were generally designed to do one row at a time. Row spacing in fields that required cultivation had to be wide enough for a horse to pass between rows and this made multi-row implements awkward and impractical.

Tractors, trucks and farm machinery grew larger. Each increase in horsepower and capacity gave the potato grower the ability to expand his potato acreage and produce a larger percentage of tubers in his rotation cycle.

Potato diggers were slow to improve. They were designed primarily to unearth the potatoes and leave them exposed on top of the ground, to be picked by hand and put in field bags. Harvesttime required many hands and people who did not do field work any other time of year were recruited to pick potatoes in the annual September-October race against the freeze-up. The pickers filled their field bags about half-full and they were loaded on wagons to be hauled from the fields and dumped in potato cellars. The soft soil in the harvest fields frequently made three teams of horses necessary to pull a wagon load of potatoes from the field. Once on the road, two teams could usually pull the wagon to town for storage or shipment. When trucks became available, the transportation problem of hauling crops to market lessened.

As harvest labor became harder to get, machinery designers began to improve diggers. The use of chain link conveyors to separate field dirt from potatoes soon led to a more complex machine that elevated the potatoes in bulk to the height of a potato truck and eliminated hand picking and field bags. Space was provided on some harvesters for people to stand so they could remove vines, trash, clods of soil and field stones. These potato harvesters revolutionized field work by eliminating hand picking and the lifting of bagged potatoes for loading. The flood gates were open for big operations and potato fields got larger and larger.

The Mormon pioneers in Franklin County dug irrigation canals and brought the water to their crops by gravity flow. From lateral ditches, the water was diverted to flow down the rows of potato plants in fields. For many years, nearly all of the irrigation in the west was done by gravity. Water had to originate from a reservoir or dam at a higher

High school girls harvested a bountiful potato crop in 1943.

elevation and the land to be farmed had to be level for efficient gravity irrigation.

A major breakthrough was the development of sprinkler irrigation. The facts are not available as to who did the first irrigation with sprinklers in Idaho, but by the late 1940s the trend had begun. A major factor was the development of light-aluminum sprinkler pipe that could be moved from one part of the field to another. These are called handlines. One of the big advantages of sprinkling is that it is no longer necessary to have flat ground. The system adapted to the gently rolling hills of much of Idaho's unreclaimed desert areas and made possible the addition of thousands of new acres of potato ground.

Pumps were used to create the pressure for sprinkling and were usually powered by an electric motor or an internal combustion engine. At first the water was pumped from irrigation ditches.

Another major breakthrough in technology was the development of pumps powerful enough to lift the water from deep wells and supply pressure to operate a sprinkler system. Geologists and well drillers were finding that most of the Snake River Plains area had vast resources of underground water. An aquifer of great size and value was discovered.

The Idaho Power Company and Utah Power and Light Company were quick to anticipate the power demand that land reclamation and deep-well pumping could create and developed additional generating capacity to handle the load. New irrigation developments sprouted like seed potatoes in June and each year there were more and more potatoes to sell.

Sprinkler potatoes proved to be of more uniform quality because soil moisture and soil temperature could be controlled with greater accuracy. Sprinklers worked better on light soils and their use greatly reduced irrigation runoff which carried silt and other undesirable substances back into rivers.

Agricultural chemicals have also contributed greatly to the technological revolution in the potato industry. The availability and use of chemical fertilizers alone has increased yields and quality of potatoes greatly. Insecticides, herbicides and fungicides have given the grower new weapons to fight insects, weeds and disease. Mechanization and the availability of custom application service have enabled growers to handle larger farming operations with the utilization of modern agricultural chemicals.

The industry is now engaged in the development of an integrated pest management program aimed at the reduction of dependence on chemicals and involving biological controls by utilizing natural enemies of pests and disease organisms. By 1991 Idaho's potato production had grown to 122.2 million cwt for which growers received $489 million.

Another technological advancement that has contributed greatly to the Idaho potato industry is the mechanically refrigerated railroad car and its companion in motor carriers, the mechanically refrigerated semi-trailer. The latest development in the transportation of frozen foods is the CO^2 refrigerated rail car in which the freight car is charged with liquid carbon dioxide to keep the load frozen solid for periods as long as 14 to 16 days if necessary.

Without the availability of refrigerated transportation, it would be impossible to move the huge tonnage of frozen potatoes to market which is now being shipped. In addition to frozen products, mechanically refrigerated cars and trucks are also used to ship fresh potatoes with more accurate temperature control and reliability than the old ice bunker box cars that were used for so many years.

The development of computers has impacted the agricultural industry as it has almost every productive activity in the western world. A computerized system called Automatic Defect Removal has enabled potato processors to eliminate most of the hand labor of trimming defects from potatoes that are to become French fries and other processed products.

Use of automated controls on nearly every phase of processing has likewise accomplished savings in labor cost and tightened tolerances for higher quality.

On the farm, controls of temperature, humidity and air movement in potato storage buildings are now under the ever-alert monitoring of computers as are some sprinkler irrigation systems. Scheduling of irrigation is also optimized by government-owned computers that calculate the amount of moisture plants have used and how much has evaporated by temperature and wind. Growers use the information to regulate the quantity of water they put on crops accordingly.

A new irrigation system is currently under development in which individual sprinkler nozzles can be automatically controlled to supply more or less water to each section of the field as the center pivot system passes over it. The water-need information comes from infrared aerial photographs which show the relative wetness or dryness of every part of the field. Scanning the photograph into a computer enables it to automatically change application rates of each nozzle on the sprinkler system to provide exactly the amount of water needed.

Computers have steadily increased their usefulness to fresh shippers in optical sizing and grading functions. Machines that fill consumer-size bags now depend on electronic brains to get the weight of the contents exact without underweights and a minimum of overweights.

Other mechanical aids have also become available to the Idaho potato industry. Processors now steam peel potatoes as opposed to the caustic process which was universal twenty years ago.

Large vacuum equipment is being used to suck out the potatoes in a "hot spot" which may have developed in a storage building, thus leaving the healthy tubers undisturbed and removing those that could spread the rotting process to the entire pile.

Planters and harvesters have been improved to do their jobs better with special emphasis on bruise prevention in the harvesting process. Operating a potato harvester is a job that requires a well-trained person, however, and the problem of bruising potatoes, although somewhat improved, is far from solved.

The new technology adopted by the Idaho potato industry has required huge investments by growers, shippers and processors. Labor savings have resulted, but the most significant benefits have accrued to consumers in higher quality and uniformity of potatoes bought in supermarkets and eaten in foodservice outlets.